BELIEFS

Pathways to Health & Well-being

Robert Dilts
Tim Hallbom
Suzi Smith

METAMORPHOUS PRESS
Portland, Oregon

Published by

Metamorphous Press
P.O. Box 10616
Portland, OR 97296-0616

Copyright © 1990 by Robert Dilts,
Tim Hallbom and Suzi Smith
Cover Art, Book Design & Editing by Lori Stephens
Printed in the United States of America

Dilts, Robert
Beliefs: pathways to health & well-being /
by Robert Dilts, Tim Hallbom, Suzi Smith
p. cm.
Includes bibliographical references.
ISBN 1-55552-029-4
1. Neurolinguistic programming. I. Hallbom, Tim.
II. Smith, Suzi. III. Title
RC489.N47D55   1990
158'.1--dc20   90-31473

Dedication

To my mother, Patricia
who taught me about living
to my father, Robert
who taught me about life
to my wife, Anita
who taught me about loving
and to my son, Andrew
who taught me about being.

Robert Dilts

Acknowledgements

The list of people to be acknowledged in a work such as this is both broad and deep. The individuals that contributed to both the intellectual and operational background of the material presented here span not only my own life time, but also the entire course of recorded history. People like Aristotle, Sigmund Freud, Konrad Lorenz, Fritz Perls and others who set the stage for our current understanding about the human psyche deserve to be acknowledged. John Grinder and Richard Bandler, the two creators of NeuroLinguistic Programming have contributed immensely to the work that follows; both as the originators of many of the principles and the techniques from which these processes were derived, and also as personal mentors and friends of mine. Other people whose work has influenced this material include Milton Erickson, Gregory Bateson, and Timothy Leary; I had the tremendous privilege of being able to study with each personally.

I would also like to acknowledge the late Virginia Satir, whose work has contributed to this material. My colleague, Todd Epstein, who serves as my sounding board for almost all of my ideas has contributed to these materials constantly. I would like to thank the host of my NLP colleagues, network of trainers, the many individuals that I've had the opportunity to assist, facilitate, and learn from in my own work with beliefs, in my own striving to more fully understand and promote the process of human well-being, choice, and creativity. Last, but certainly not least, my mother who has served as my primary guide through the experiential and intuitive understanding and development of the material to follow.

Robert Dilts

There are some additional acknowledgements that we would like to add. Dave Young contributed a transcription to the chapter on allergies, Michael and Diane Phillips of Anchor Point helped with editing suggestions, Paula Walters provided support originally, The Eastern Institute of NLP who shared transcripts from workshops, and Steve and Connirae Andreas of NLP Comprehensive who shared audio and video tapes of workshops conducted by Robert, as well as providing insights on editing. In addition, Dale L. Longworth for indexing and Lynn Turner for typing. We would also like to thank our many friends, students and colleagues who have encouraged us to continue on with this work.

Suzi Smith
Tim Hallbom

CONTENTS

MAPPING ACROSS SUBMODALITIES
PROCESS SUMMARY

Introduction

Change is a multilevel process . . .
We make changes in our environment;
Changes in our behaviors through
which we interact with our environment;
Changes in our capabilities and
the strategies by which we direct and guide
our behavior;
Changes in our beliefs and value systems by which we
motivate and reinforce our guidance systems and maps;
Changes in our identity of which we select the values
and beliefs we live by;
Changes in our relationship to those things which are
bigger than us, those things that most people would call the
spiritual.

This book is about gaining more choices at a particular
level of change—the level of beliefs. The purpose of this
book is to provide conceptual and interactive tools necessary to understand and gain more choices within the belief
systems that guide our behavior in the world around us.

I first began exploring the processes involved in changing beliefs in earnest when my mother had a recurrence of
breast cancer in 1982 with a fairly wide degree of metastasis

and a poor prognosis for recovery. It was in helping her on her dramatic and heroic road to recovery, elements of which are described in this book, that I became intimately associated with the effects of beliefs in relationship to a person's health and in relationship to the other levels of change involved in making complete and lasting behavioral change.

The first "Beliefs and Health" workshop was conducted in December, 1984. Most of the concepts and techniques described in this book are a result of that program, the programs that have followed, and also of the work that I have done with particular individuals who were engaged in both life threatening and life transforming changes. While the roots for the concepts and techniques presented in this book have reached widely and deeply, it draws most heavily on the principles and techniques of NeuroLinguistic Programming. The sources for the material in the book are primarily advanced NLP seminars in which the issue of beliefs was being presented and dealt with as an advanced level skill.

The book is written in such a way that you can associate into being a participant in an actual workshop. Imagine that you are there, watching the demonstrations, listening to the questions and answers, and participating in the discussions and exercises.

The primary purpose of the book is to provide the "how to's" of belief change—although I hope you, as a reader, will find inspiration as well, within the concepts and examples of the people that make up this book.

I should also point out that this is such a rapidly developing area in NLP that we already have enough updates and new techniques to fill a second volume. Thus I recommend that you approach this book as a way of expanding your own beliefs about the possibilities and methods involved in the process of lasting change, as opposed to a simple description of techniques or procedures.

1

Beliefs:
Identification And Change

In 1982 my mother had reached a transition point in her life. Many things were changing for her. Her youngest son was leaving home and she was having to deal with what his leaving meant to her. The law firm my father had been working with was splitting up and he was going into business for himself. Her kitchen, the heart of her home, had burned down and she was feeling frustrated and upset about that because the kitchen was "her place" and partly represented who she was in our family system. On top of it all, she was working long hours as a nurse for several doctors, and had commented that she was "*dying* to take a vacation."

In the midst of all these stresses of change in her life, she had a recurrence of breast cancer that metastasized to her skull, spine, ribs and pelvis. The doctors gave her a poor prognosis and basically said they would do what they could to "make her comfortable."

My mother and I spent four long days working with her beliefs about herself and her illness. I used every NLP technique that seemed appropriate. It was exhausting work for her. When we weren't working she ate or slept. I assisted my mother in changing a number of limiting beliefs and helped her integrate major conflicts that had developed in her life because of all the life changes that had occurred. As a result of the work we did with her beliefs, she was able to make dramatic improvements in her health and elected not to receive chemotherapy, radiation treatment, or any other traditional therapy. At the time of the writing of this book (7 years later) she is in excellent health, and there have been no further cancer symptoms. She swims one-half mile several times per week and is living a happy full life that includes trips to Europe and roles in TV commercials. She's an inspiration for all of us about what is possible for people with life-threatening illnesses.

The work I did with my mother was pivotal in my development of NLP models to work with health, beliefs, and belief systems. The models that I use now have evolved considerably in the past seven years, and will be the focus of this book.

Even before I worked with my mother I had become intrigued with belief systems when I recognized that, even after doing an NLP intervention "successfully," some people with whom I was working still didn't change. In exploring why, I often discovered that the people held beliefs that somehow negated the change they wanted. One typical example of this occurred when I was presenting to a group of special education teachers. A teacher raised her hand and said, "You know, I think the NLP strategy for spelling is great and I use it on all my students. It just doesn't work for me." I tested her and discovered that in fact the NLP strategy *did* work for her. I could teach her to spell a word until she could spell it frontwards and backwards correctly. However, because she didn't *believe* that she could spell, she would discount her new ability. This belief allowed her to override all the evidence that she could, in fact, spell.

Belief systems are the large frame around any change work that you do. You can teach people to spell as long as they're alive and can feed back information. However, if people really believe they can't do something, they're going to find an unconscious way to keep the change from occurring. They'll find a way to interpret the results to conform with their existing belief. In order to get the teacher, mentioned earlier, to use the spelling strategy, we'd have to work with her limiting belief first.

A Model For Change Using NLP

When working with any limiting belief, your goal is to get from your present state to your desired state. The first and most important step is to identify your desired state. You need to have a clear representation of your outcome. For instance, if you are working with a smoker, you'll need to get him to consider who he'll be and what he'll do in his relationships, work life, recreation, etc. when he no longer smokes. Once you've helped someone set an outcome, you've already started the change process because his brain is a cybernetic mechanism. This means that once he is clear about his goal his brain will organize his unconscious behavior to achieve it. He'll begin to automatically get self-corrective feedback to keep him on track toward his goal.

I heard about an example of this recently. Someone wrote a master's thesis at an Eastern university in 1953 on goal setting. The person writing the thesis found that only 3% of the students had written lifetime goals. Twenty years later, in 1973, someone checked with the surviving members of the class of '53 and found that the three percent of the students with written goals made more income than all the rest of the class put together. This is an example of how your brain will organize your behavior to achieve a goal.

After you've identified what you want, you can then gather information about your current situation; your present state. By contrasting and comparing your present state with your desired state, you can determine what abilities and resources you need to achieve your desired state.

Formula for Change

I'd like to present my simple NLP formula for change: **Present (problem) state plus resources equals desired state.**

Present State + Resource = Desired State

This is essentially the process you use with all the specific techniques that NLP has developed over the last 17 years. Sometimes you run into difficulty in adding resources to the present state. Something in the person's thinking interferes. You then have a model that looks like this:

Present State + Resources = Desired State

⇧ ⇧ ⇧

Interferences

(Including Limiting Beliefs)

Recognizing and Working with Interferences

I sometimes humorously label interferences "internal terrorists" who sabotage all your best efforts. Unfortunately, you can't go in and arrest the "terrorist" because it's a part of you that needs to be evolved and incorporated rather than destroyed. Consider an interference a communication that *another set of resources* is needed before you move on towards your desired state.

The most typical kind of interference is the type that exists *within* the individual. Sometimes people are trying to gain some desired outcome, but do not consciously realize that they are getting certain positive benefits from the problem that they're trying to overcome. Let me give you some examples of how this works.

A woman might have difficulty losing weight because she's afraid that if she does, then people might be sexually attracted to her. Losing weight would create anxiety because she doesn't know whether she'll be able to handle those situations gracefully.

When a man who is sick gets a certain type of attention from his family that he doesn't normally receive, *that* can become a motivation for staying sick. When he is well he feels taken for granted, and doesn't get the attention that he wants.

I remember a fellow I worked with who had cancer of the liver. When I asked if there were any parts of him that objected to becoming healthy again, he felt a hesitancy. A part of him was concerned because he had gathered all his friends together for a grand farewell party, where everyone bared their souls and cried. This part felt that if he got well, he couldn't possibly live up to all that incredible emotion. It would all be downhill from there because he had that peak experience that was predicated on his dying. Not being able to live up to this peak experience represented an interference. I had to deal with that interference before adding any other resources.

Interferences can take one of three forms. The first is that some part of the person doesn't *want* the change. Often the person is not consciously aware of this part. I was working with a man who wanted to quit smoking and every conscious part of him agreed. However, there was an unconscious "15 year old" part of him that thought if he quit smoking he'd be too much of a conformist. If he quit smoking he'd no longer be himself. We needed to take care of this identity issue before giving him more appropriate ways of being an independent person. In order to create change, you have to congruently *want* the change.

A second kind of interference is when the person doesn't *know how* to create a representation of change or how he'd behave if he did change. You have to *know how to* move from present state to desired state. I once worked with a boy who had an auditory spelling strategy and couldn't spell. He tried to spell by sounding out the letters. Of course he couldn't spell very well, because to spell effectively you need to see the word and get a feeling of familiarity or unfamiliarity. I taught him the NLP visual memory spelling strategy, which gave him the "know how" to spell.

This brings us to the third kind of interference. A person needs to give himself the *chance to* use his new learnings. There are some common ways that people don't give themselves the chance to change.

A person often needs the time and space for the change to take place. If someone tries an effective strategy for losing weight and doesn't see results within a few days, he hasn't given himself a "chance" to change. So, just giving yourself time can give you the chance you need.

Another kind of "chance to" example was demonstrated when Tim Hallbom and Suzi Smith were once talking to an instructor from a graduate school about how to help people create change in their lives. The instructor said "I've read about the NLP phobia technique in *Using Your Brain—For a Change* but I'd never use it because it's just a "quick fix." She thought for change to be worthwhile it had to be a long, painful process. Tim and Suzi said, "We've used the process lots of times and seen it last for years." She said, "I don't care if it lasts; it's *still* a quick fix." This instructor was a person who *wanted* to be more effective as a people helper, but couldn't learn *how to* because she wouldn't give herself a *chance to* because of her fixed and limiting belief about how change should occur.

Summary

In summary, you can create change by:
1. Identifying the present state;
2. Identifying the desired state;
3. Identifying the appropriate resources (internal states, physiology, information or skills) that you need to get from present state to desired state; and
4. Eliminating any interferences through using those resources.

You've got to *want* to change, *know how* to change, and give yourself the *chance to* change.[1]

Additional Elements That Influence Change

There are four additional elements that relate to influencing change and are a part of wanting to change, knowing how to change and giving yourself a chance to change. These elements are: (1) physiology, (2) strategies, (3) congruency, and (4) belief systems. Any change that you make is in some way going to be influenced by each of these. Let me divide it this way:

- Physiology and strategies have to do with knowing *"how to."* How do you *do* a particular behavior?
- Congruency and beliefs have to do with *wanting to* do something or giving yourself the *chance* to do it. You have to be able to make a full personal commitment and not be fighting yourself or fighting other people in being able to accomplish it. You also have to be able to believe that it's possible for you.

1. Physiology

Physiology, in the sense that I'm using the term, has to
do with accessing the right states in your body, to get your
physiological processes in the appropriate modality (see,
hear, feel) to do a particular thing. Let me give you some
examples of what I'm talking about in relation to physiology. I've been studying speed-reading for a number of years
and have found that those who read the fastest make the
most of physiology.

One man I studied does the following to get himself
ready to read: he takes a book, sets it down and stands back,
getting ready to pounce on it. He approaches it, grabs it,
looks it over, turns it around in his hands quickly, and
stands back again. THEN, he *really* gets into it. He cracks
his knuckles, loosens his collar, takes a deep breath and
grabs it again as he sits down and gets into reading quickly.
Try that one out . . . it's a little earth-shaking. Once you go
through that whole process of getting pumped up, you
can't read slowly! (slowly) On the other hand, if you're
trying to speed read and you're going (sighs . . .) and you're
sitting back all relaxed . . . it's going to be a little more
difficult to read quickly.

Let me give you another example. When you teach
somebody to visualize, as a part of a change process, you
may have to do more than tell them to make a picture. You
may also need to get them into the appropriate physiology.
For instance, if a woman comments that she doesn't know
why she can't make a picture, notice her posture. If she is
slumped back, breathing deeply in a kinesthetic posture or
has her head tilted down and to the left, it's no surprise that
she can't make a visual image because her body is in a
posture that is associated with feelings and hearing, not
seeing.

My metaphor for physiology (which extends on down
into subtle physiological changes, like your eyes moving up

to make pictures and moving down for feelings and sounds), is that of a television or radio tuner. There are stations transmitting television waves through the room you're in right now. A television set has a specific physiological set-up that allows it to pick up those waves. When you turn to channel 7, it picks up one frequency of these incoming waves over the others, with minimal interference from the others.

People operate in much the same way. If I want to make internal images, I look up and right, I make my breathing shallow, and my body shifts so that it's more upright and I'm able to make a picture.

Occasionally if you turn to channel 3, you'll get interference from channel 4. That happens in your mind sometimes, too. You have the picture of what you want, but you've got the wrong voice attached to it . . . you've got a voice that's saying, "No, you can't do that." So you get noise from another channel—your auditory channel. Using your physiology correctly allows you to be able to do some particular behavior and get the outcome you want.

2. Strategies

In NLP "strategies" is the word used to describe how people sequence their internal and external pictures, sounds, feelings, smell and taste to produce a belief, a behavior or a thought pattern. (We refer to the five senses as representations or modalities. We never experience the world directly—we "re-present" it to ourselves through internal images, sounds and voices and kinesthetic feelings.) An effective strategy uses the most appropriate representations in the most appropriate sequence to achieve a goal.

For example, when the goal is spelling a word correctly, good spellers will almost always make a remembered picture of the word, and then check their feelings to make sure the picture is "right." Poor spellers use ineffective strategies, such as trying to sound out the word phonetically, or trying to construct a picture of the word from its sound. Neither of these strategies work well for consistently spelling correctly. In the case of speed-reading, as long as people sub-vocalize, their reading speed will be limited to how fast they can talk. Regardless of what physiological state they're in, they're going to reach a limit in their speed. If they say the words to themselves, instead of seeing them, it slows them down because words are sequential. To change to a faster reading speed, they would need to see the words and form images of their meaning directly.

One thing that makes a person a good athlete or a good dancer is the ability to watch people do something, and then step right into it themselves. You might think they're good because they're better coordinated than most people. What allows them to be better coordinated? It is the map that they're using in their mind—the sequence of representations and the submodalities that they use? (Submodalities are the qualities or smaller elements within each modality. For example, a few of the submodalities in the visual representational system include brightness, clarity, size, location and focus; in the auditory system, volume, tempo, location of sound; kinesthetic, pressure or duration of touch. Changing submodalities or the sequence of representations will change your subjective experience of any event, often dramatically.)

All of us have "talents," not because we're smarter or have better genes, but because we can build robust representations for a particular skill or behavior quickly and efficiently. To illustrate this, think of some subject in school you learned quickly and easily and were talented in. Then think of one you struggled with. Notice the difference in the way you represent each of these. The difference in your "talent" has to do with the strategy that you used.

3. Congruency

Congruency occurs when you make a full conscious and unconscious commitment to some outcome or behavior. Eating properly and maintaining an appropriate weight is easy if "all parts" of you want to, you utilize the right physiology, and have good strategies for selecting and eating your food. It's very difficult, however, if you're concerned that if you eat in a healthy way it'll reduce the enjoyment in your life. You can get in the most appropriate physiology and learn effective strategies, but you won't eat in a healthy way if you don't congruently want to.

Incongruence is often the reason some behaviors are so hard to change. Issues like smoking, excessive drinking, weight loss, etc. are problematic because some part of you wants to change but another part (often an unconscious part) of you derives some positive gain from the behavior you want to change.

Once when I was working with a woman who wanted to lose weight I asked, "Can you tell me what it would be like if you were thin again?" She said, "I know exactly what it would be like. I'd look like I did when I was a beauty queen and didn't like myself." It's no wonder that she had been struggling for years and not losing weight. When she was a beauty queen, she wasn't in control of her own life. Being able to eat what she wanted, when she wanted it, etc. was, for her, tied into being in control of her life. Being thin meant she had someone regulating everything that she did and judging her. For her, this was far more involved than "just losing weight."

When you put your resources and energy into a goal that you're not congruent about, some part of you will fight the change and probably keep it from happening. Earlier, I humorously called this part the "internal terrorist." If you're congruent about what you want, it's much easier to find many ways to reach your goal.

If you're in a larger system, like a corporate environment and there are incongruencies in goals or values between the people working there, any project that you try to implement will provide an opportunity for conflict. When congruency is an issue, you can hire the best people, use the best consultants, buy the best equipment, acquire the best learning materials, and still miss getting the results you want.

Internal conflicts (incongruencies) come in many forms. There may be congruency issues between what you *should do* and what you *want to do*. For instance, you may think that you *should* quit smoking for health reasons, but you really *want* to keep smoking because it's the only thing that you really do for yourself.

There can be congruency issues about what you *can do* or *can't do*. You know that you *can* ask your boss for a raise because you think you're deserving, but you just *can't* quite get yourself to do it. "Can't" beliefs are harder to identify than "should" beliefs because the person is telling you, "Yes, I *do want* to do it, I just *can't*." It *seems* like the person is really congruent (especially to them), but something stops them from doing what they want. It generally seems to the person that they are being sabotaged from within. (The "terrorist" emerges.) "Can't" beliefs usually come from unconscious imprints. Imprints will be discussed in Chapter 4.

4. Beliefs and Belief Systems

Beliefs represent one of the larger frameworks for behavior. When you really believe something, you will behave congruently with that belief. There are several types of beliefs that need to be in place in order to achieve your desired goal.

One kind of belief is called *outcome expectancy*. This means that you believe that your goal is achievable. In relating this to health, it means that you believe it is *possible* for people to get over something like cancer. When people don't believe a goal is possible (like getting over an illness, for example), they feel hopeless. And when people feel hopeless, they don't take the appropriate action to get well again.

No Outcome Expectancy = Hopelessness

Another kind of belief is called *self-efficacy expectancy*.[2] This means that you believe that the outcome is possible and that *you* have whatever it takes in order to reach your goal. In relating this to health, this means that you believe that you have the necessary resources to heal yourself (even if you believe you need to reorganize those resources).

A person may believe that a goal is possible for *others* to achieve, i.e., people can get over cancer, but not possible for himself. When the person believes he doesn't have what it takes to accomplish his healing, you'll typically find a sense of helplessness. No self-efficacy expectancy equals a feeling of helplessness and helplessness also leads to inaction.

No Self-efficacy Expectancy = Helplessness

Both kinds of beliefs are essential to taking action to achieve desired health outcomes. When a person feels *both* hopeless and helpless, he becomes apathetic. This can present a real problem when he's working with illnesses that are potentially life-threatening. When you're doing belief work with someone else, you may need to work with one or both of these beliefs.

If you ask a person to rate his own outcome expectancy and/or his self-efficacy expectancy, you'll often find an incongruity. For example, when you ask "Do you believe that you'll recover from your illness?" you'll frequently get the verbal reply "Of course," while the person is shaking their head in nonverbal disagreement. If you work with a person based only on what he *says*, you'll miss half the message. When someone offers you an incongruent message like that, you want to work with the conflicting parts using the "Negotiation Frame" (which we will discuss later in Chapter 5) to build appropriate beliefs of self-efficacy and outcome expectancy.

Response Expectancy and the Placebo Effect

Another belief that is useful to know about is called *response expectancy.*[3] Response expectancy is what you expect to happen to you either positively or negatively as a result of the actions you take in a particular situation. The placebo effect illustrates an example of response expectancy.

The placebo effect occurs when a person responds positively to a physiologically inactive "drug"—a flour pill, a milk substance capsule, sugar pill or some other inert ingredient. You give a placebo to someone, tell them that it will produce a certain effect, and sure enough, it often does. Placebos often have a very high success rate. On the average they work as well as the genuine drugs in about one third of the cases.

I reviewed a considerable amount of research a number of years ago because Bandler and Grinder wanted to market placebos. They thought they would put them in bottles and label them "Placebos." Accompanying them would be little booklets that included statements that placebos have been proven to be effective in the treatment of different illnesses in "x" number of cases. You could look down the list and find your chances of success based on the statistics.

My review turned up some interesting statistics. In the case of pain, research has shown that placebos can work as well as morphine in 51-70% of the patients.[4] Another study looked at placebos from the opposite point of view.[5] In this study, the researchers wanted to find out how well the placebo responders reacted to real drugs, so they gave them morphine. They found out that 95% of the placebo responders *did* respond in a positive way to the morphine. In comparison, only 54% of people who did not respond to placebos got relief with real morphine—a difference of 41%. People with a high response expectancy for relief got relief. With this kind of data you have to wonder about the efficiency of certain medicines.

Another interesting study showed that the response expectancy (the belief about what the drug would do) was the major deciding factor influencing results.[6] This was a study involving alcohol where the subjects were divided into four groups:

1. People who were told they would get alcohol and did get alcohol;

2. People who were told they would get alcohol and got a placebo;

3. People who were told they were not going to get alcohol but did; and

4. People who were told they were not getting alcohol and didn't get alcohol.

The two groups that were told they were getting alcohol had almost identical responses. Their responses were very different from those of the people who were told they weren't getting alcohol but did. Both of the groups who were told they were getting alcohol started craving more of it. The group who was told they were getting alcohol but didn't, had no such reaction. Males who were told they were getting alcohol (whether they received it or not) tended to have slower heartbeats than normal when they were put into what were termed "sexually anxiety producing" situations. The groups who were told they were not getting alcohol (whether they really did or not) had increased heart beats in the same situations.

The researchers concluded that there is both a pharmacological effect from the drug *and* an expectancy effect. The study also points out that the response expectancy is the most important element, at least with those behaviors affected by alcohol. Another study pointed out that males and females responded differently in terms of physiology. The researchers said they could not find a way to account for this by the pharmacological effects of alcohol, or differences of physiology between males and females. They concluded that the responses were functions of beliefs.[7]

In essence, these studies point to the same thing. The placebo effect (the person's response expectancy) is a very important component of behavior and of change.

Many beliefs have to do with expectancy. If you don't expect to get well from an illness, you won't do all the things that can help you get better—especially those things that may be difficult. In other words, if you don't believe your outcome is going to be there when you get through working on your issue, or you don't believe you have what it takes to get the outcome, you're not going to do what it takes to achieve your goal.

How Are Beliefs Changed?

Beliefs are not necessarily based upon a logical framework of ideas. They are, instead, notoriously unresponsive to logic. They are not intended to coincide with reality. Since you don't really know what is real, you have to form a belief—a matter of faith. This is really important to understand when you are working with a person to assist him in order to change his limiting beliefs.

There is an old story described by Abraham Maslow that illustrates this. A psychiatrist was treating a man who believed he was a corpse. Despite all the psychiatrist's logical arguments, the man persisted in his belief. In a flash of inspiration, the psychiatrist asked the man "Do corpses bleed?" The patient replied, "That's ridiculous! Of course corpses don't bleed." After first asking for permission, the psychiatrist pricked the man's finger and produced a drop of bright red blood. The patient looked at his bleeding finger with abject astonishment and exclaimed: "I'll be damned, corpses *do* bleed!"

This is a humorous story, and yet I've worked with people in a number of instances who share something in common with the man in this story. This is especially so if the person has a potentially terminal illness. The belief is, "I'm already a corpse—already dead, and no treatment will help me. The most intelligent thing for me to do is to stop fighting the inevitable." That's a tough belief, because at the present state of our knowledge no one else can tell you whether you will get better or not.

There was an interesting study I read about a few years ago, but I don't recall the specific source. A woman had interviewed 100 "cancer survivors" in hopes of finding out what these survivors had in common. She described a cancer survivor as someone who had been given a terminal diagnosis of cancer with a poor prognosis for recovery, but who was still alive and healthy, enjoying life ten or twelve years later. Interestingly enough, she could find no common patterns in the treatment received by these people. Different people received different treatments, including chemotherapy, radiation therapy, nutrition programs, surgery, spiritual healing, etc. However, there was one thing that these survivors all shared: they all believed that the method of treatment they were getting was going to work for them. The belief, not the treatment, made the difference.

Types Of Beliefs

1. Beliefs about Cause

You can have beliefs about what causes something. What causes cancer? What causes a person to be creative? What makes your business successful? What causes you to smoke? What causes you to fail at losing weight? The answer you give will be a statement of belief.

You might say, "I have a bad temper because I'm Irish," or "Ulcers run in my family," or "If you go out without a coat you'll catch a cold." The word because (actual or implied) often indicates a belief about cause.

Some friends of mine who do business consulting were working with a large company that was being plagued with illness. Many employees had colds and the flu. The CEO of the company informed my friends that they were doing extensive repairs on the air conditioning and ventilation systems of their new building because they figured faulty ventilation was causing the employees' illnesses. My friends later discovered that the office where everyone was sick had gone through four major reorganizations in the past seven months. What caused so many people in one office to have the flu? Was it the stress of reorganization, the ventilation system, or germs? Beliefs about cause come from the filters of your experience. If you believe that "X" causes something, your behavior will be directed toward making "X" happen or stopping it from happening if it has negative consequences.

2. Beliefs About Meaning

You can have beliefs about meaning. What do events mean, or what is important or necessary? What does it mean if you have cancer? If you have cancer does that mean you are a bad person and are being punished? Does it mean that you are out to kill yourself? Does it mean that you need to make changes in your lifestyle?

What does it mean if you can't quit smoking? Does it mean that you are weak? Does it mean that you are a failure? Does it mean that you just haven't integrated two parts yet?

Beliefs about meaning will result in behaviors congruent with the belief. If you believe that your difficulty in quitting smoking has to do with two unintegrated parts, you'll probably work towards integrating them. If you believe that it means you're weak, you may not take action towards integration.

3. Beliefs About Identity

Beliefs about identity include cause, meaning and boundaries. What causes *you* to do something? What do your behaviors mean? What are your boundaries and personal limits? When you change your beliefs about your identity it means you are going to be a different person somehow. Examples of limiting beliefs of identity are, "I am worthless," "I don't deserve to succeed," or "If I get what I want I will lose something." Beliefs about identity are also the beliefs that may *keep* you from changing, especially because you are often not conscious of them.

Let's contrast beliefs about identity with phobias. Phobias are usually behaviors that don't fit with your identity. This is one of the reasons that they are generally so easy to change. Richard Bandler once worked with a woman who had a phobia of picking up worms. So Richard said, "Do you have to pick up worms a lot? You're not a worm farmer or something are you?" She said, "No, it's just that being afraid of picking up worms doesn't fit with who I am." Richard was able to help her eliminate her fear quickly.

This fear was *outside* her definition of her own identity. That fact is going to make this issue easier to deal with than some issue that *is* part of her identity. I don't know how many times I've been working with a client when she suddenly realizes that she *will* have the change she's been asking for and she says, "I can't do that because I wouldn't be *me* anymore."

The effect of belief upon identity can be substantial. For example, I was doing some change work with a woman in a workshop in Europe who had some fairly severe allergies. When I checked to make sure the change would be ecological for her, she froze up. It turned out that she is an allergist. To change her allergy via a simple NLP process would have blown out her identity as a medical practitioner. It would require a major change in her professional identity.

To summarize, beliefs may be beliefs of meaning, of identity and of cause. They may have to do with the world around you, including other people, or they may be about your "self" and your identity.

Beliefs are largely unconscious patterned thinking processes. Because they are mostly unconscious patterns, they are hard to identify. There are three main pitfalls that you need to stay mindful of, and avoid, when you are trying to identify a person's beliefs or belief systems.

Pitfalls In Identifying Beliefs

1. Fish in the Dreams

The first of the three pitfalls is what I call the "fish in the dreams" phenomenon. This notion comes from a comic radio show that David Gordon (a well known NLP author, developer and trainer) told me about that used to be on a Los Angeles station. A man portrayed a psychoanalyst who had a belief that having fish in your dreams was the root of all psychological problems. People would come to him and start telling him about their problems and he'd interrupt and ask . . .

Psychoanalyst: "Excuse me, but you didn't happen to have a dream last night, did you?"

Client: "I don't know . . . I guess maybe I did."

Psychoanalyst: "You didn't dream about fish, did you?"

Client: "Ah . . . no . . . no."

Psychoanalyst: "What was your dream about?"

Client: "Well, I was walking down the street."

Psychoanalyst: "Were there any puddles along the gutter?"

Client: "Well, I don't know."

Psychoanalyst: "Could there have been?"

Client: "I suppose there could have been water in the gutter or something."

Psychoanalyst: "Could there have been any fish in those puddles?"

Client: "No . . . no."

Psychoanalyst: "Was there a restaurant on the street in the dream?"

Client: "No."

Psychoanalyst: "But there could have been. You *were* walking down the street weren't you?"

Client: "Well, I guess there could have been a restaurant."

Psychoanalyst: "Was the restaurant serving fish?"

Client: "Well, I guess a restaurant could be."

Psychoanalyst: "Ah ha! I knew it. Fish in the dreams."

One of the problems, then, in identifying beliefs is that you as the helper, tend to find substantiation for *your* beliefs in someone else. I know a therapist who had been sexually abused as a child—she was always trying to uncover abuse in people that she worked with. She managed to find sexual abuse in most of her clients—whether it was actually there in their personal history or not.

2. The Red Herring

When people tell you about their beliefs often you'll get logical constructs that they've invented to make sense out of certain behaviors that they engage in. Freud talked about the notion of free-floating anxiety (anxiety caused by an unconscious conflict). According to Freud, all that the person is aware of when having this problem is the feeling of anxiety. So he makes up logical reasons why he feels the way he does. His logical reasons have nothing to do with his anxious feelings.

I call these logical constructs "red herrings." If you've ever worked with an "obsessive-compulsive" person you've probably encountered this phenomenon. For example, a woman might have explanations about microbes and why she feels bad. Her explanations generally don't have anything to do with where those feelings are coming from. Freud claimed they always developed from repressed sexual feelings. I find, instead, that the feelings she is experiencing often comes as a result of internal conflicts which are, indeed, unconscious, but often have nothing to do with sex.

3. The Smokescreen

There is one more problematic behavior that can keep you from identifying a belief, which I call the "smoke-screen."

Often when you are working with a belief, especially a belief that has to do with someone's identity (or an issue that is very painful to deal with), it will be hidden by smokescreens. You can identify smokescreens when the person suddenly starts blanking out, or begins to discuss something irrelevant to the process you're doing. It's as if the person has entered a cloud of confusion. It's important for you to be aware that people will often "fog out" just at the point where you're getting to something that is *really* important. Like an octopus or squid that squirts a cloud of ink to escape a predator, the person usually fogs out because she—some part of her—is afraid. She's dealing with a belief that has to do with her identity—a belief that is painful or unpleasant, and she doesn't want to admit it, even to herself.

Often someone will say, "I just draw a blank when you ask me that." If you use a feeling to search back through time to an early imprint experience she may say, "I can remember this early experience but it doesn't have anything to do with my problem." At other times she suddenly starts telling you about some utterly unrelated experience; or she just gets really confused and can't answer at all.

To summarize, the three major problems in identifying beliefs are:

(1) The *"fish in the dreams"* phenomena, which are reflections of your own beliefs;

(2) The *red herring,* which is creating some explanation for your feelings because you're not aware of what really causes them;

(3) *Smokescreens,* where you block out or disassociate off some belief structure so you will be protected from confronting it.

Identifying Beliefs

Once you've managed to avoid the pitfalls, how do you identify beliefs? Obviously, when you're working with an unconscious belief, you can't ask the person you're working with, "What is the belief that's limiting you?" because he doesn't know. You will get one of two responses; he'll either answer you or he won't. If he answers you, he may be offering you a red herring or putting up a smokescreen. If he doesn't answer you he's reached an impasse because he has no idea. Beliefs are often hard to define for a person because they are so much a part of everyday experience, it's hard to step back and identify them clearly. You can often find limiting beliefs by working through smokescreens. When the impasse occurs you might get responses like: "I don't know . . ." or "I'm sorry, I just go blank," or "This is crazy; it doesn't make sense." Paradoxically, those are the kind of answers that you want, because they let you know that you're really close to eliciting a limiting belief.

Limiting beliefs are often stated in ways that violate the meta-model.[8] The most common language patterns that indicate beliefs are *modal operators* and *nominalizations*. These might typically have to do with what the person *can* and *can't* do; *should* or *shouldn't* do; or *ought* or *ought not* to do. You might also hear, "I am this way," "I am a poor speller," "I am a fat person." These statements indicate identity beliefs that limit the person's thinking about themselves, and what they can do to change.

Beliefs may also be stated as cause-effect phenomena, that are often stated in "if/then" kinds of statements. "If I don't say my prayers, I'll be punished." "If I assert myself, then I'll get rejected." "Just when I start to succeed, everything turns to garbage."

Finally, beliefs can often be identified by finding a problem situation the person has unsuccessfully tried to change using a variety of methods—including NLP. When you ask, "What does it *mean about you* that you haven't been able to change this?" you sometimes get an identity belief statement in response. You can ask the person, "What do you want instead, and *what stops you from having that?*" You can anchor the response you get (a bad feeling, a blank, whatever), and search it back to the experience that laid the foundation for the belief. The ways of identifying beliefs will become more clear as we demonstrate some of the various ways you can work with beliefs using NLP.

If you're going to change your identity or a limiting

belief you hold:
(1) You've got to *know how to do it.*
(2) You have to *be congruent about wanting your outcome.*
(3) You also have to have the belief that it's *possible* for you to make the change.
If any one of these things are missing, the change won't be complete. You can want to do something, believe you can do it; but if you don't know how, you don't have the physiology, or you don't have the right strategy, you will experience difficulty. Furthermore, you can have all the abilities, all the training and everything you need to be effective at something, but if you're incongruent about it or if you don't have the belief you can do it, you won't be able to get the change you want.

The Structure Of Beliefs And Reality

How do you *know how* a person believes something? Does he believe things through feelings? And if he believes something through feelings, how does he get to the feelings? Does he have a feeling as a result of something he sees or hears?[9] What is the basic orientation in his strategy?
I don't know how many people I run across who say . . "I don't know, I've *told* myself ten million times I'm not going to *feel* that way when I go into that situation again," or "I've promised myself, when I go talk to that person I won't feel uptight, but when I get there, I still feel that way." Promising himself that he will change doesn't work because his strategy for getting the *feeling* doesn't have anything to do with what he *tells* himself. It has to do with either his self-*image* and the feeling, or a comparison of two pictures or some other strategy. Other people will say, "Well, I've tried *visualizing* things, over and over, but *something tells me* it won't work. I don't understand it, either, because I'm really good at making clear pictures. I can see myself getting

a promotion and doing well, but something tells me I'll fail." If you know how to watch and listen for these internal connections, you'll find out how a person has structured his limiting beliefs.

Often people get feelings from internal images they make. It's useful to know that sometimes the most important thing is the *kind* of picture that it is. Occasionally there is a very subtle "difference that makes a difference" in submodalities that determines whether you're going to have a strong feeling about something or not. (Chapter 3 of this book has a demonstration on how to elicit those differences.) It's important to gather enough high quality (behavioral) information to know precisely how to intervene.

Many NLP Practitioners get into a bind because they labor under the belief that NLP is supposed to be so fast that if it takes them more than 20 minutes, they're doing it wrong. That belief can help them increase their speed. However, sometimes it's worth spending the extra time finding the most critical elements of a limiting belief. There's nothing necessarily important about *how* they're going to add resources. The process of adding resources, regardless of the technique used is less important than knowing *what* to change. The next two chapters deal with how to uncover the way a person has constructed their reality and their beliefs. Having the ability to identify the structure of a person's thinking gives you the ability to know exactly how to intervene effectively.

ENDNOTES

1. Joseph Yeager, a well known NLP trainer and author defined these three components necessary for effective changes; (a) to want to change; (b) to know how to change; and (c) to get the chance to change.

2. A. Bandura, "Self Efficacy: Toward a Unifying Theory of Behavioral Change," *Psychological Review 84* (1977), pp. 191-215.

3. Irving Kirsch, "Response Expectancy as a Determinant of Experience and Behavior," *American Psychologist* (November 1985), pp. 1189-1201.

4. (a) F.J. Evans, "The Placebo Control of Pain," in J.P. Brady et al., *Psychiatry: Areas of Promise and Advancement* (New York: Spectrum, 1977).

(b) "The Power of a Sugar Pill," *Psychology Today* (1974, 1977) pp. 55-59.

(c) "Placebo Response: Relationship to Suggestibility and Hypnotizability," Proceedings of the 77th Annual Convention of the APA (1969), pp. 889-890.

5. L. Lasagna, F. Mosteller, J.M. von Felsinger & H.K. Beecher, "A Study of the Placebo Response," *American Journal of Medicine, 16* (1954), pp. 770-779.

6. (a) G.A. Marlatt, et al., "Cognitive Processes in Alcohol Use" in *Advances in Substance Abuse: Behavioral and Biological Research* (Greenwich, CT: SAI Press, 1980), pp. 159-199.

(b) Bridell, et al., "Effects of Alcohol and Cognitive Set on Sexual Arousal to Deviant Stimuli," *Journal of Abnormal Psychology, 87*, pp. 418-430.

(c) H. Rubin & D. Henson, "Effects of Alcohol on Male Sexual Responding," *Psychopharmacology, 47*, pp. 123-134.

(d) G. Wilson & D. Abrams, "Effects of Alcohol on Social Anxiety and Physiological Arousal: Cognitive vs. Pharmacological Processes," *Cognitive Therapy and Research, 1* (1977), pp. 195-210.

7. *Ibid.*

8. See John Grinder and Richard Bandler, *The Structure of Magic I* (Palo Alto, CA: Science and Behavior Books, 1975) for a complete description of the meta-model.

9. See John Grinder and Richard Bandler, *The Structure of Magic II* (Palo Alto, CA: Science and Behavior Books, 1976).

2

Reality Strategies

 A common childhood experience is to claim that something happened in sensory experience that was really a dream or fantasy. Lots of adults still aren't sure whether or not a powerful experience they had as a child was real or imagined. Another common experience is when you have been absolutely certain you told someone something and they claim you didn't and later you realized you rehearsed it in your mind but never actually talked with them.

As human beings, we will never know exactly what reality is, because our brain doesn't *really* know the difference between imagined experience or remembered experience. The same brain cells are used to represent both. Because of that, we have to have a strategy that tells us that information received through the senses passes certain tests that imagined information doesn't.

Try a little experiment. Think of something that you could have done yesterday but know you didn't do. For example, you could have gone shopping yesterday, but you didn't. Then think of something you know you did do—like go to work or talk with a friend. Contrast the two in your mind—how can you determine that you didn't do one and did do the other? The difference can be subtle, but the qualities of your internal pictures, sounds and kinesthetic feelings will be different. As you contrast your imagined experience with your real one, check your internal experience—are they located in the same place in your field of vision? Is one clearer than the other? Is one a movie and one a still picture? Are there differences in the qualities of your internal voices? The quality of information that we have in our senses is somehow coded more precisely for the real experience than the imagined one, and that's what makes the difference. You have a "reality strategy" that lets you know the difference.

Many people have tried to change or re-program themselves by visualizing themselves being successful. For all the people who naturally use this as a strategy, it will work fine. For all the people that use a voice that says "You can do it," this visual programming won't work. If I want to make something real for you, or convince you about something, I've got to make it fit *your* criteria for your reality strategy. I have to make it consistent with the qualities of your internal pictures, sounds and feelings. (These qualities are called submodalities.) So, if I assist you in changing your behavior in some way, I want to make sure that it is going to fit in with you as a person. By identifying your reality strategy, you can determine precisely *how* you need to think to be convinced that something is legitimate enough for you to do.

Reality Strategy Demonstration

Robert: Joe, would you come up here so that I can demonstrate how I elicit and work with a reality strategy? What we're looking for in Joe is a sequence of internal representations or checks he goes through to determine what is real. As you watch and listen to this demonstration, I'd like you to keep a couple of general strategy elicitation rules in mind. The first rule is to engage the person as fully as possible in the here and now as you are eliciting his strategy. I'll want to engage Joe in an ongoing example of his reality strategy rather than ask him to remember something. I'll want to use present tense language to keep him associated in the experience.

The second rule involves contrast. I'll want to contrast an experience Joe knows is real with one he knows is imagined. By using contrast, I can identify what is *different* in his thinking process—I don't care about what is the same. It will be the differences that we can test to make sure we have his reality strategy, versus some other strategy.

(*To Joe.*) We're going to start by having you think about a simple action you took that doesn't have any emotional content. What is something you did yesterday that you know you did?

Joe: Traveling on the train and bus to get here.

Robert: Now pick something that you could have done, but didn't do.

Joe: Have an ice cream sundae.

Robert: You could have had an ice cream sundae, but you didn't. That fits completely in the realm of possibility.

Joe: Oh, actually, hold on a second . . .

Robert: You did have one, huh? (Laughter) What did you have on top of your ice cream sundae?

Joe: Just granola.

Robert: So you had granola. What's something that you could have had on it, but you didn't?

Joe: I could have had hot fudge on it.

Robert: You could have had hot fudge. One of the nice things about strategies is that it *doesn't matter what the content is.* Believe me, when we start determining what is real for Joe and what is not, the distinction of hot fudge or granola is going to be just as important as any identification of reality. Whether it's a hot fudge sundae or getting in a fight with someone you're close to, the content doesn't really matter. The process will be the same.

(*To Joe.*) How do you know that you took the train and the bus and that you had granola instead of hot fudge? How do you know that you really did one and not the other?

(*To Group:*) Watch. He's showing us the answer.

Joe: Well, I know I had granola because I went through a process of remembering it, and having remembered it, I know that I must have done it.

Robert: What he's doing is interesting, because I've elicited a lot of reality strategies from people, and usually I get this one later in the elicitation. He said, "Well, I thought about the granola first, so logically, I must have had that."

(*To Joe.*) How do you know that you went through this process I mean sitting right here, right now?

Joe: (Eyes up and left) Well, when you asked me to come up with something that I did yesterday . . .

Robert: You visualized . . .

Joe: Yeah. (Eyes up and left again)

(*To Group:*) As I mentioned, there's a *sequence* of processes. I saw Joe do more than make a picture, although that was the starting point. Often you don't question your first reality check because when you think about what you did, there's one thing that comes to mind, and it seems like that's all there is. You don't question *one* picture in your mind, but you may question the reality if you get two different pictures.

(*To Joe.*) I'll ask you what you really did yesterday, and this time I want you to visualize hot fudge.

Joe: I didn't have hot fudge.

Robert: Right. But I'm going to ask you to picture it. That's how you "know" the difference. Initially, when I said, "What did you do yesterday?" you saw granola rather than hot fudge. I'm going to ask you to go back through the same process because I think you have more mental checks than

just a picture of granola on ice cream. What I want you to
do now is to make two pictures; make the one of ice cream
with granola, and another one with hot fudge, and make
them look like each other. I'm going to say, "What did you
have yesterday?" and I want you to visualize hot fudge with
the same internal visual qualities as the granola.

Joe: I just did while you were talking.

Robert: OK. What did you have yesterday?

Joe: (Incongruently) Ah . . . I had the ice cream with . .
ah, hot fudge on it.

Robert: Did you really?

Joe: No.

Robert: OK. How do you know?

Joe: That's a good question, because I can make a pretty
good picture of ice cream with hot fudge. I've had it plenty
of times. It's not an image that just comes out of nowhere.
It's a part of me, in a way.

Robert: But you still know which you had. This is important. Now you have two images that are equally clear. You
can see one as well as the other. If I say, "What did you
have?" you can see either one. How do you know which one
you really had?

Joe: That's a good question. It's not just from the picture, I guess.

Robert: Think about it. Are you sure about which one
you had.

Joe: Ah . . . yeah.

Robert: Good. (Laughter) What makes you sure?

Joe: I can contextualize it.

Robert: That's good, too.

(*To Group*:) So there's another piece. Typically, the first
response for reality is whatever comes up on the first association to the question. Even though we're talking about
a trivial instance here, we can put this in the context of
beliefs. You say to someone, "Are you a good speller?"

"No, I'm not a good speller."

"How do you know that?"

"Just never have been."

The first association is whatever comes up. What Joe said next is, "It's not just the picture that I come up with, now there's a context around it."

Let's find out what context means. My guess is what we're going to discover—judging from Joe's accessing cues—is an internal movie.

(*To Joe:*) Maybe you saw yourself pulling out the granola. The granola is not going to suddenly turn into hot fudge just because you can clearly see a still picture or an image of a hot fudge sundae. Is that it?

Joe: Absolutely. Good guess.

Robert: OK. What do you see up there? (Points up to Joe's left, where Joe is moving his eyes.)

Joe: Just supper time, along with the whole context of the other food I ate. My wife was there, but there wasn't any hot fudge in that experience.

Robert: Can you put hot fudge in?

Joe: Yeah, OK.

Robert: You're picturing it?

Joe: It's all in my mind's eye.

Robert: Now, what did you have after dinner on your sundae last night?

Joe: Granola.

Robert: How do you know that? When I asked you, did you see them both? How did you make that determination?

Joe: Because I heard myself say it.

Robert: Oh, because you *heard* yourself say it. That's interesting. There's a voice in your head that tells you what's real.

(*To Group:*) I'm going to push this a little bit, and we'll eventually get to a point where you'll see a change happen. You will see momentary confusion.

(*To Joe:*) You have a voice . . .

Joe: While we were sitting here, I just *told* you . . . (Joe emphasizes the word *told* indicating an internal voice.) It was more like a habit. I already *told* you that I had granola and so . . .

Robert: It's a habit?

Joe: I must have said it at least a half a dozen times.

Robert: What would make it just as familiar to have talked about hot fudge?

Joe: I would have done it. I'd have memories of doing it.

Robert: Repetition is one way to make something real and familiar. How many times would you need to see it and tell yourself you had it? Half a dozen?

Joe: I don't know.

(*To Joe*.) I'm going to ask you half a dozen times what you had on your sundae yesterday, and I'd like you to visualize the picture you have of hot fudge and say "hot fudge." Are you willing to do this?

Joe: Sure.

Robert: What did you have yesterday on your sundae?

Joe: Hot fudge.

Robert: Was it good?

Joe: Very good.

Robert: What did you have yesterday, again?

Joe: Hot fudge. I had to rush making it, because I was in a hurry getting out.

Robert: It was what that you had?

Joe: Hot fudge.

Robert: Let's wait a little bit . . .

Joe: It's more of a peanut butter fudge, actually. (Laughter)

Robert: Was it very hot or . . .

Joe: It's best if you let it cool a little bit, so that it doesn't melt the ice cream as much. It was very good.

Robert: OK. How are they matching up, now? What did you have?

Joe: I had hot fudge.

Robert: OK. (Laughter)

(*To Group:*) We only did a few trials. This is the same strategy that people use with affirmation tapes. If you repeat something often enough, it will become more real for you. (*To Joe:*) What did you have last night?

Joe: I had granola.

Robert: How do you know that, now?

Joe: The pictures are different . . .

Robert: Think of granola. Really think of it. I want you to visualize it. OK. That's good. Now, visualize the hot fudge. Really visualize it. I noticed something different about the physiology that Joe is displaying. When you visualize those two things, Joe, I want you to look at them side by side. Do they go side by side or does one overlap the other?

Joe: I only thought of them separately, so far.

Robert: When you visualize the granola, where does it appear in your visual field in your mind's eye?

Joe: About here. (Gestures to left center)

Robert: About there (Repeats Joe's gesture). Where is the picture when you visualize the hot fudge?

Joe: I think it was almost the same place.

Robert: Here? (Gestures to right of center slightly). Is there anything qualitatively different about the two pictures? Compare them now.

Joe: I've just gone through a process to make them the same—so, no.

Robert: OK. I want you to actually put your eyes over there and visualize the hot fudge there. (Gestures left of center). OK? Now, take the granola and put it over here. (Gestures to right of center). Got it? Which one did you have? (Long silence, look of confusion on Joe's face and then group laughter)

Joe: . . . I had the . . . granola.

Robert: Good.

(*To Group:*) The point is that now we're starting to see a little lag in this processing. Of course, you can take this to an extreme and I'm not really into doing that. The reason that I'm doing this with Joe is not to confuse him about reality, but to find out what those checks are. Let's say I want Joe to change something, and I want to convince him that this is a real change that he can have. If I really want Joe to have as much of a choice about some new behavior as he had about some old behavior, I need to identify his reality checks.

The only thing Joe has to rely on to determine reality are the representations (pictures, sounds, and feelings) that are stored in his mind.

Since your brain doesn't know the difference between a constructed image (one that you've made up) and a remembered one, you can imagine how confusing it gets when you're dealing with things that happened 10 years ago. Or what if you're dealing with a dream and you're not sure if you really had it or made it up? How do you know what is real?

Joe: The submodality distinctions seem really important for me in determining the difference. My contextual movie of the hot fudge isn't as bright, it isn't as focused, and . . .

Robert: (*To Group*.) He's telling us about the next steps to take. Rather than continuing this as a demonstration, Joe can explore this further in the upcoming exercise.

I am asking you to do the following exercise because it is often useful to explore a person's reality strategy when you are working with his beliefs. Joe relies on some pictures, sounds, and feelings that flash into his mind in a fraction of a second. Whenever any of you make decisions about what you believe, you don't sit down and analyze what's happening in your brain. Are the submodalities a certain way? Is there a movie or voice there? etc. One movie might have feelings with it, and the other movie might not. You won't get a chance to consciously analyze these fleeting thinking processes. Typically, you'll notice the first picture

or voice that comes to mind and that's what seems real . . .
the one that's been imprinted in you most strongly. That's
the reason why I think it's important to find out about your
own reality strategy. . . . Not everyone's going to have the
same strategy that Joe has, and it's useful to find out how
you determine what's real.

Reality Strategy Exercise

I'd like to ask everyone to do an exercise using the
following format.

Part I:

(a) Pick some trivial thing that you did, and something
you could have done but didn't do. Make sure that the thing
that you could have done but didn't do is something that
is completely within your range of behavior. If you could
have put peanut butter on your ice cream, but you don't
like peanut butter on your ice cream, you wouldn't really
have done that. Pick an example like Joe did, where you've
done one thing a number of times and yet you've also done
some other thing a number of times. The only difference
should be that you "actually" did do one of them yesterday.

(b) Determine how you know the difference between
what you did and what you could have done. What you
come up with first will typically be the most obvious reality
check. You might have a picture of one and not the other.
After you make the picture, you may notice other things
about it. Joe went through submodality differences. He
made a movie about it and filled in some other pieces. He
said the one he did was brighter.

Part II:

(c) Pick two things that happened during your childhood and determine how you know that they were real. You're going to find that it is a bit harder to determine what happened back then. In Joe's case, we took something that happened less than 24 *hours* ago, and we were able to shift realities. When you consider something that happened 24 *years* ago, it's an even more interesting decision process because your pictures will not be as clear and may possibly be distorted. Sometimes people know the real things that happened because they were fuzzier than the things they made up.

(d) Start making an event that you didn't do like the one other that you actually did. After you get the pictures of the one the person might have done, looking like the pictures of the experience the person actually did do, shift representational systems to auditory or kinesthetic. For example, Joe switched to the ongoing context. He said, "I can check, because just a few minutes ago when you first asked me which one was real, I told you it was the granola and I can remember that." We haven't changed that memory yet.

Be careful as you begin to change the thing that you didn't do to be represented like the thing you did do. I'd like you to at least get to a point where you have to really think about which experience was real, like our example with Joe.

The object here is not to confuse your reality strategies, but to find out what reality checks exist for you. Remember, we're eliciting a strategy, not trying to destroy it. Note: The person who acts as the responder can put a hold on the process whenever you want to. If the process starts getting scary (which it sometimes can), you may get a swishing sound, or maybe you'll feel a spin. (There are various kinds of signals that a person can get.) When someone else is eliciting and playing with your reality strategies, it is appropriate to ask them to stop when you get uncomfortable.

Discussion

Let me share a process with you that John Grinder and Richard Bandler taught us when we were first learning about NLP. They had us take a number of experiences that we did on a particular day (either successfully or unsuccessfully), and locate the point where a decision was made. We'd pick three alternative resourceful behaviors that we could have done in each of those experiences and run them through our reality strategies, making each behavioral choice as full, radiant, and moving (using the same submodalities) as our reality strategies.

Whether each behavior was successful or not, we'd develop more behavioral choices. If it was a negative experience, we'd often find that there was a simple thing we could have done to have been more resourceful. I'd recommend this process for negative experiences. Go through the entire negative experience, making sure everything works out in a positive way. The next time you encounter a similar situation to the negative experience, instead of going back and unconsciously associating to what you did the last time (and the time before that and the time before that), you now have a decision point with new choices. You'll be responding in a new way.

One of the claims that I make is: *"Success is as much a limitation to creativity as is failure."* This is because when you remember a success, your memory often becomes really strong and you get a good feeling about it. You are likely to keep doing the same thing over and over again without exploring other options. You get to a point where you stop being creative and get stuck, because you've run into a new situation where your old behaviors don't work *and* you don't have new choices.

The U.S. automobile industry is a good example. It had been very successful for many years but now seems unable to respond quickly and effectively to changing needs and foreign competition. I heard someone say that if the automobile industry had changed as much, and had come as far since it started as the computer industry has, that a Cadillac would cost $2.75 and go a million miles on a tank of gas. The computer industry has changed and refined to fit new realities and needs, but American automobile innovation *has been a slow process that relied on its own success* for a long time.

Questions

Man: When you were working with Joe, you had him visualize having hot fudge several times. Would you say more about that kind of repetition?

Robert: Let me answer by telling you about a client.

I remember working with a nurse who had gotten so depressed that she planned to poison herself and her two children. She told me she'd do anything to feel better. I said, "First, you want to change your state; let's find out if you have any good memories." Of course, like most depressed people, she said no. Notice that I didn't really ask for a memory, I asked for a *decision*. In essence, I said, "Sort back through your memories, find one that you would *decide* is positive, and tell me about it." That's a complex question to answer and it doesn't really have anything to do with faulty memory. It has to do with making judgments and decisions about what's positive. Since I wanted to change this woman's state, I said, "What would it be like if you could now breathe differently and sit up, look up and right and imagine something positive?"

Her eyes looked up and she started visualizing something positive. I saw a shift in physiology that looked very positive. Then, suddenly, she stopped, looked back down and returned to the depressed state. I asked her, "What happened? Did you hit a bad memory or did something come up that got in your way?" She replied, "No." I asked her what made her stop doing it. Her reply was, "It feels funny to put my eyes up there. It's very unfamiliar." Think about that response. Here's a person whose bad feeling made her so desperate that she was going to poison her children. Yet she stopped doing something that was making her feel good because it was unfamiliar. So, I asked her how she would know if it was familiar, She said, "I would have done it before." I had her look up once, twice, three times and finally after about 10 times, it felt pretty familiar for her to do that. It was an important breakthrough in her therapy. Having done something before is a powerful convincer confirming the reality of either positive or negative experiences. Repetition is one way that people make something seem real and familiar.

Joe has a part of him that can determine which of his experiences is real now, because in the ongoing context of eliciting his strategy (this doesn't have anything to do with yesterday anymore), he told us that he had granola more times than he's had hot fudge. Therefore, repetition is very convincing.

What does it mean if someone tells you they haven't been able to do something like sing on key for 30 years? Is that proof that they can't? *No. It just means that they've been trying to do it the wrong way for a long time.* It doesn't mean they *can't* do it. I'm marking this out as significant, because repetition of experience is so important. One of the reasons that it's important is that there's a process that all of us go through called threshold. Threshold can apply to beliefs, reality strategies or learning strategies. If you have a little metal strip and you bend it back and forth, it will go back pretty much the same way it started. It goes back to the same form that it had before, even though it's been bent a little bit. If I take that metal strip and repeatedly bend and twist it, the strip will eventually break. Once it snaps, no matter what I do, it won't go back to the way it was before. The metal strip has been pushed over a threshold. Nothing I do now will get it back unless I recast it or weld it. I suddenly put the strip through a radical change by bending it and twisting it. The same thing happens when you put a person through such a dramatic shift that makes his past seem a lot less real than what it has been up until now. That's a function of the way your brain works.

Woman: How do reality strategies relate to something like New Behavior Generator?

Robert: When doing New Behavior Generator, you visualize yourself doing something with new resources, then step into the visualization. If you don't filter that new experience through your own reality strategy, then you're just pretending. On the other hand, what's the difference between pretending and really changing? If you pretend long enough, it will seem as real as anything else.

Man: It was really important for me to hold onto my "reality" and not change it.

Robert: Have you ever had an experience where you did doubt reality?

Man: Yeah.

Robert: The goal here is *not* to be confused about your reality strategy. If you wanted to change that strategy, we'd go to the time when you doubted reality and have you re-experience it with the appropriate resources. Many of the beliefs we have acquired were installed by the time we were 5 years old by your parents, significant other people and possibly by the media. These are people that often don't know about how to install good reality strategies. A lot of your beliefs were installed in your brain before you had well developed reality strategies. Those of you who acquired good reality strategies were either lucky, or else you had bad experiences with the alternatives. You eventually figured out how to install good ones.

Even though most of us are sure about our reality, you'd be surprised at how much of your reality you've actually built. You most likely believed in Santa Claus at one time, but you've changed that. You still might find yourself dealing with beliefs and realities that were programmed in at a time when you didn't have resources for determining high quality information. For example, a child often confuses their dreams for reality. Sometimes people have such strong reality strategies that it limits them from using their imaginations as a resource also. It's a very delicate balance, even when you know what you're doing.

Occasionally people will "fuzz out" bad experiences, pretending that they really did not happen. They downplay them. Other times, people will take experiences and exaggerate them beyond what really happened.

What if you take an event that someone thinks was real, that set them in a direction in life 25 years ago, and change it? When you do that you may need to first work with the belief, "I've wasted 25 years of my life because of the beliefs I've acquired."

As an example, a lady I worked with had been through a lot of physical and emotional problems. These problems were severe enough to create a survival issue for her. Her problem stemmed from an internal "voice" that was giving her all kinds of trouble. We gave her resources concerning a past experience to change her body image and gave the part of her that created "the voice" new resources. When we integrated all these resources together, she became really, really sad, like she had lost something. When I asked her what was going on, she said, "All my life, my goal has been to survive. Surviving has always been a challenge. Now that I have all these resources, it's like part of me is gone. What am I going to live for now?" This is not a bad place to get to with a client, because then you can say, "What do you *want* to live for? What would be a worthwhile mission? What would be nice, instead of just having to survive all the time?"

When you do really good work and help a person create change that's pervasive, the mission question is probably going to come up. And it's not always something you're going to know about ahead of time. If you work with this possibility before you work with other issues, and future-pace new possibilities for the person, it makes your work easier.

How many of you fight your own reality strategy and get stuck when you try to change your own behavior? I've heard people say, "I'd give anything to be different, but I don't want to fool myself." They're saying, "If I filter this new belief for behavior through my reality strategy in such a way that it becomes as real for me as the other things that I do, I'll be fooling myself." You are damned if you do and damned if you don't. That is a double bind. Even if you're checking reality on something that's trivial . . . like whether you had hot fudge or granola, you'll often run smack up against some real important beliefs or conflicts.

The value in understanding reality strategies is not that of determining what really happened in your life. Instead, it allows you to set up a series of decision checks or behavior checks to pass through before you're willing to believe that something new is true, or before you're willing to actually take action. You're not going to take action on something unless it's clear, or unless it fits into the overall scope of who you are, etc.

3

Belief Strategies

 Belief strategies are the ways in which we maintain and hold beliefs. Like reality strategies, they have a consistent pattern of pictures, sounds and feelings that operate largely unconsciously. Belief strategies are a set of evidence procedures you use to decide whether something is believable or not. This kind of evidence is usually in the form of sub-modalities—the qualities of your pictures, sounds, and feelings. Try an experiment for yourself. Contrast something you believe with something you don't believe. Notice the differences in the qualities of pictures, sounds, and kinesthetic feelings. How does your brain code the differences? A common difference is the location of the pictures, but there will be other differences as well.

Belief strategies are different from our "reality strategies," because we cannot test them with sensory based reality checks. Because they are so highly patterned, they can last a lifetime. This is fortunate, because without these strategies, our understandings of ourselves and the world would not be stable.

The problem is that belief strategies work as automatically and as durably for limiting beliefs as they do for beliefs that propel us toward our potentials. Luckily, they have a definite structure that can be elicited, so they can also be changed at the most basic levels of thinking through conscious intervention.

Belief Strategy Demonstration

Robert: Judy, think of something that you wish you could believe about yourself, but you don't. Do you have an issue like that?

Judy: Well, I was working on weight, because that's a big issue for me . . .

Robert: A real heavy one, I bet. What do you now believe about that?

Judy: What do I now believe? I have a lot of conflicting beliefs. I use all the shoulds and can'ts and apply them to my weight. I have a lot of conflict.

Robert: What's one of the limiting "can'ts"?

Judy: That I can't lose weight.

Robert: So you can't lose weight. We're going to fill this out a little bit . . . so to speak. What is something that you know you can do?

Judy: I can use NLP methods with clients.

Robert: First, let's do a basic comparison. We might be able to find all the information by doing a comparison.

I want you to think about losing weight for a moment. (Judy slumps down, sighs, and she looks down and to her left with muscle tension around her mouth.) Now, think about doing NLP with a specific client, maybe a time that you particularly validated a success. (Judy's shoulders lift, the tension leaves her face and she looks up.) OK.

(*To Group:*) You can see that there's a pretty dramatic difference in physiology; accessing cues as well as the rest of the physiology.

There are two reasons I asked her to do this. First, we'll know whether or not she's changed her belief about her ability to lose weight based on what we see. What are we going to see? We're not going to see the first physiology, we're going to see the second physiology. We now have a way of testing whether or not she's changed her belief. The physiology differences will provide us with an accurate unconscious test of our work. The second reason is to provide a contrast of present state with desired state and to sort out what is different in her physiology.

(*To Judy*:) Now I'd like you to do some comparisons in your mind. When you think about losing weight, how do you think about it?

Judy: It's a struggle.

Robert: It's a struggle. (*To Group*:) And she repeats the contrast that we saw in her physiology beautifully. One of the nice things about working with people is that they tend to be very systematic in their patterns. Now we've seen this physiology a few times. It looks like a pattern.

(*To Judy*:) What makes it a struggle? (She repeats the physiology associated with her difficulty in losing weight, looking down to her left, the eye movement that indicates internal dialogue.)

Robert: I believe you. It wouldn't be something that you say to yourself, would it?

Judy: It probably would be.

Robert: What do you say to yourself?

Judy: That I have to work hard at it. The only way I can lose weight is to count calories and keep track of everything I put in my mouth. But then I know that I'm going to be hungry and uncomfortable.

Robert: So, when you've decided, you count calories— even though it's hard and you say it's a struggle. What's the conflict?

Judy: Well, I do that for so long, and then I stop doing it.

Robert: What makes you stop doing it? Right now when you think about it, what's the conflict?

Is it a conflict because you think it's going to be hard and you don't want it to be hard? Do you think it's going to be hard but it won't work?

Judy: I'd like to forget about the whole issue and just let my body take care of itself. That's what I would like.

Robert: And you don't believe that you can do that?

Judy: That's right. I believe *other people* can, because I've helped other people do that. But *I* can't do it. (Gestures with her right hand, while her left hand is still.)

Robert: I want to ask you to pay attention to a couple of other things.

(*To Group*:) Notice that as she's talking about the conflict, there's an asymmetry in her gesturing. She says, "I wish I could just drop the whole thing and let my body do it" and uses both hands—a symmetrical gesture . . . then she used an asymmetrical gesture when she says she can't do it. Those asymmetries are usually very, very telling in indicating internal conflicts. For example, when someone says to me, "I want to really be aggressive," and he's got his right hand just sitting flaccid, it probably means that a part of him wants him to be aggressive and another part of him doesn't. Calibrating to body symmetry is very helpful. It's not that I think that every time somebody isn't gesturing symmetrically they're in a conflict; instead, it's a cross-check that I use. If I don't see symmetry, I'm going to keep checking for when they gesture with one hand versus the other as they talk about their problem. In Judy's case, we'll check to see what she is saying and how she is thinking about her "struggle" as she gestures.

(*To Judy*:) When you say you "have to count calories," are those the words that you hear in your head?

Judy: (Looks up and to her left, indicating a visual memory.) Well, that's the way I've been successful in the past.

Robert: So, when you think about counting calories, are you seeing something in your mind? Are you talking to yourself about it, or what?

Judy: Yes. I see the little calorie counter book, and I'm looking up things, and writing them down . . . (moves her eyes down and left indicating internal dialogue, then to her right, indicating feelings.)

Robert: And seeing those things, you obviously get a certain feeling or something attached to that. So, when you do that, do you get a feeling?

Judy: Yes, I do. I talk to myself too.

Robert: Now, if you just see the book and the counting of calories, does that make you have the feeling? (Judy pictures the book, slumps down and moves eyes down and right.) OK. So, just looking at that can trigger the feelings. Now let's contrast this with doing NLP with clients, the behavior Judy believes she *can* do comfortably.

(*To Judy:*) You've done NLP with other people . . . yes? (Judy immediately adopts the more resourceful physiology.) How do you know that you can do that, and it's not a lot of work?

Judy: Well, I can see it clearly in my mind.

Robert: What do you see?

Judy: I can see the person that I'm working with. I see the response and I also hear confirming feedback from my client.

Robert: This is the interesting thing. There's a phenomenon that I jokingly refer to as therapist's or consultant's syndrome. You have all these skills that are developed around seeing and hearing other people. Yet, when it comes to you, you can't see and hear yourself—so you get lost. You don't know what to do. It's not because of anything that you're doing wrong. It's just that you can't see or hear yourself and give yourself feedback. It has nothing to do with an inadequacy on your part.

(*To Judy:*) So you see the other person and gather

information about their problem. How do you know that you can do something to help them? How do you know what to do?

Judy: I get a feeling about it.

Robert: OK, so you get a feeling. In this internal picture, where you are working with someone successfully, do you see them from your own eyes? Are you associated into the experience? Or are you watching yourself as well in a disassociated way?

Judy: It's from my own eyes, just like I'm there with them.

Robert: How is this picture different from the book picture where you're counting calories?

Judy: It's a wider picture. It's a bigger picture in the sense that it has more scope.

(*To Group:*) See the symmetry?—Judy gestures with both hands in describing her client situation.

Judy: When I think about counting calories, I just see the book and that's all.

Robert: So, you just see the book. Anything on the book?

Judy: I can see the words and the cover and the colors . . . it's like a color photo.

Robert: But when you see the client? (She shifts physiology and the group laughs.)

(*To Group:*) Could be a pattern. We get two hand symmetry with the client, and then asymmetry with calorie counting; here she just gestures with her left hand.

(*To Group:*) Let me summarize what we've accomplished thus far. We've gathered information about Judy's belief that she "can't lose weight." When asked about losing weight she makes a little still picture of a calorie counting book and gets a negative feeling. Then a voice comes in and says, "Other people can lose weight." We've also noticed an asymmetry in her gesturing—when she talks about losing weight, counting calories and hard work, she gestures with her left hand. When she says, "But I can help other people," she gestures with her right hand. There is also a consistent posture that looks non-resourceful that she adopts whenever she thinks about trying to lose weight.

We've contrasted this with something she thinks she can do—helping clients using NLP. Here we find that she makes a big panoramic picture and hears the client just like she's there all over again. She also adopts a resourceful posture and gestures symmetrically with congruent hand gestures.

What we have been doing is finding the *patterns* in her behavior that are present with each belief. At this point, as I'm gathering information, I like to have my client identify another belief about her abilities—another belief about what she *can* do. I'll gather the same kind of information about her physiology, her eye movements, her posture and her internal images, voices, and feelings so I can cross-validate my information. I want to find out what patterns are the *same* in terms of these qualities between the belief that she can help someone using NLP and some other useful belief about "what she can do."

Judy: I thought of one as you were talking. I made a major change about how I felt about my mother . . . which generalized to everything in my life.

Robert: How did you do that?

Judy: (Laughing) I went to an NLP practitioner.

Robert: What did this practitioner do? What changed in your thinking about your mother? I mean, *you* made the changes; this person just facilitated that for you.

Judy: It was how I felt about my relationship with my Mom that changed.

Robert: The NLP practitioner didn't just say, "Change a feeling," and it changed. Something that you did inside made the feeling change.

Judy: Actually, what she had me do was write a letter. So I guess that I was talking to myself.

Robert: What did it change about your perception?

Judy: It helped me get in touch with a feeling that was there when I was . . . (Judy looks up and to her left.)

Robert: Are you seeing anything?

Judy: Yes, I see the whole scene when this happened.

Robert: So, you're seeing this person . . .

Judy: No, I'm seeing myself writing this letter.

Robert: So, you're watching yourself write the letter, disassociated, as if from a third party position?

Judy: Yes.

Robert: And you really believe that you've changed your attitude toward your mother? Does this mean you can change your attitude about people in general?

Judy: Yes, because I *see* that I can in a lot of areas of my life.

Robert: Because you *see* that ability in a lot of life areas.

(*To Group*:) One of the things I've heard her say a couple of times that shows as a *similarity* about both of these is that there's something about a "big picture." She says, "I can see the *whole thing*," instead of just parts of a picture, like in the image she made of the calorie counting book. Notice the difference between a myopic focusing on one little thing versus seeing the whole scene. She gets a lot less information from a small, still picture than she does from a whole scene.

(*To Judy*:) Do you have the whole picture about losing weight, or is it just this little book? You've helped other people lose weight. What allows you to help someone else lose weight? How do you do it?

Judy: Well, it depends on the situation with the person. I use various NLP techniques.

Robert: Regardless of the content, there's something that lets you know how to proceed. What is that?

Judy: I just sense what needs to be done. I'm taking in what I need to know in order to be able to do the next step. It's almost intuitive with me, but I know it's not intuitive . . (much laughter).

(*To Group*:) By the way, one of my goals in using NLP with people is to get them to operate at their intuitive level. Because if you have to sit around and think about everything you're doing, it's a lot of time and work. NLP methods validate your intuitions and help you better, that's all.

I'm hypothesizing that Judy keeps gathering enough information from a person until she suddenly sees the whole picture and that's how she knows what to do. Right now I don't necessarily want her to come up with her solution; what I want to do is to get her to *believe* that she can do it. Obviously, she's not going to lose weight sitting up here in front of us. If she believes that she can do it, I think that she has the resources she needs to be able to accomplish her goals.

(*To Judy*:) You'd like to believe that you could lose weight in the same way that you believe that you could change your feelings toward your mother, is this correct?

Judy: Yes.

Robert: What prevents you from seeing the big picture?

Judy: When I think about my weight, I get a bad feeling. Maybe if I saw the whole picture, I'd see what to do.

Robert: Let's try to make your limiting belief strategy like the strategies where you do believe you can do something. Look at yourself in your mind's eye as if you were a client that came in to see you. See yourself and the things that you've tried in the past to lose weight. In fact, hear yourself describing what you've tried. Imagine that you, "the client" told *you* all the things you've told *me*.

First of all, put the picture out in front of you. (Gestures) Do you see yourself?

Judy: I see bits and pieces of that calorie book, but I still have the feeling . . .

Robert: You still have the feeling. What do you do if you have a client and they get a feeling that they can't shake?

Judy: Well, I do little tricks. I might have them concentrate on the feeling. Then I give it a pulse and put it out there and then I have. . . . (Her physiology shifts to that of knowing what to do.)

Robert: Sounds good. (Laughter.)

(*To Group*:) I think she has all the resources. By the way, she's going to tell me how to do this.

(*To Judy*:) Can you tell me how you can lose weight?

Judy: Let's see if I can do that. (Her eyes move up to her left, then down and to her right to access her feelings.) It's such a big feeling.

Robert: So, it's a big feeling. What do you do with a client that has a big feeling? What would you have your client do?

Judy: Again, it depends. I can have them get into the "bigness" of the feeling, and then play with it. Or if it's appropriate, I might have them shrink the feeling down and make it smaller.

Robert: Which one of those would be the most appropriate for you? Use your intuition now.

Judy: Sometimes I think if I could really get into that big feeling, I'd really get a handle on my problem.

(*To Group*:) There's another thing that I'm going to do now. We can see that this isn't only a feeling; there's a picture up there too. (Gestures up and to her left.) It will be useful to find out what that picture is all about.

(*To Judy*:) Go back into the feeling now and look up. Is there anything that you see? It's OK to stay with that feeling; it may be something that you see.

Judy: I see this huge woman . . . I mean she's *huge* (Judy tenses up noticeably.)

Robert: Who is it?

Judy: Well, it influences me.

Robert: This is something that you see, and somehow this picture is connected to you? That picture is bigger than you are; it creates that big feeling which influences you. How is it connected to you?

Judy: It's what I could call an influence *on* me.

Robert: How does it exert that influence?

Judy: I feel like that huge woman is out there surrounding me all the time.

Robert: So, she's out there . . . she's like surrounding you.

Judy: Yes.

Robert: Having that piece of information, let's have you step back, move the picture away from you. See a picture of yourself surrounded by her out in front of you.

Judy: (Relaxes) OK. Yes. I like it better out there.

Robert: Now that you can see what's going on out there, what resource does the you that's surrounded by her need in order to have choices that you want?

Judy: Ah, that's interesting. I've been trying to take care of *her.* I never thought about taking care of *me.*

Robert: Well, it's *you* that needs the resources.

Judy: I need to be reassured that she is not me.

Robert: What do you need to do in order to do that?

Judy: I need to visually separate the two out.

Robert: Do that. If you need any resources, we'll add them in.

Judy: Yes. OK. I can do that.

Robert: Good. Anything else the you up there needs? (Gestures)

Judy: I'm just running through this whole business of beliefs. I *can* change the belief I've had when I separate myself from that huge woman surrounding me. I can see that my belief about losing weight has certainly not been logical since it's been based on that feeling, and whatever that personification of a huge woman is.

Robert: (*To Group:*) As we're watching Judy calibrating we're beginning to see a little bit of this other physiology coming in, the physiology associated with what Judy believes she *can* do.

(*To Judy:*) I think you have the resources you need. Probably what stopped the belief was that you didn't know what you were looking at out there. Because this limiting belief has been manifesting visually, it's hard for you to see what you need to do (Gestures) when you're surrounded by it in here (Gestures internally). It's not just chunking it down out there in the bits and pieces; you have to see the whole picture. I think that's been a big part of what was going on.

As you look at it out here in front of you, can you widen the picture? How could you separate the influence or deal with it?

Judy: I have a little mental exercise that I can go through. It's one of the techniques I would use for somebody else. I can just move them apart, then see what I need to do to lose weight. (As she is doing this process in her mind, her physiology shifts dramatically to the resourceful physiology of "what she believes she can do.")

Robert: I believe that you have the resources you need. Do you believe that you can lose weight? We can deal with specific techniques on *how* to lose weight later on. Remember, when you first thought about losing weight, there was a conflict.

(*To Group:*) I don't go on to take the next step with someone until I see a fairly clear shift in physiology like the one we're seeing here. I know I've made progress when I asked her to think about it again and she didn't fall back into the first non-resourceful physiology. I could clearly see that there is a very different strategy and physiology associated with losing weight now as compared to when I first asked her about her belief.

Identifying Belief Strategies Exercise

Let's do an exercise now. Think of something that you believe you can do and contrast it with something that limits you. Determine the difference. Then take the limiting belief and make it like the thing you believe you can do. If something stops you from doing it, find out what stops you.

The object is to make the limitation become more like the resourceful belief. Use whatever change process you can. What you end up doing may not look anything like what I did in terms of identifying the interference and adding the appropriate resource. The basic goal is to get the belief you don't believe to be as much like the one that you do believe as possible.

Discussion

Most of you found that you could identify the differences and create the desired change quickly. Some of you found good examples of significant past experiences (Imprints) that stop you. For a complete discussion of Imprints and Re-imprinting techniques see Chapter 4.

Some other people found some pretty good examples of beliefs about having to be perfect. That kind of belief can really discount the person. People who have this belief say, "I did it, but I didn't do it perfectly." You could do something perfectly a thousand times, and then if you do it wrong once, it means you didn't do it perfectly and all the successes that you have had are discounted. And of course, even though you have a success, you know it may not be "real" because if you do it wrong the next time, the rest won't count. If you compare yourself with God, you're going to end up looking shabby. A problem with this kind of belief is that your criteria for defining success is inappropriate.

Many of you probably found that the beliefs you identified involved a comparison. To illustrate, I worked with a lady who had a clear idea of what she wanted to achieve. The closer she got to achieving her goal perfectly, the worse she felt about not achieving it yet. You can imagine what a bind that was. The better she got, the worse she felt, because the closer she was to perfection, the worse she felt about that last little bit that she hadn't achieved. This person had a life pattern of starting something, doing really well at it, getting to a point where she was almost successful, and then encountering so much stress she would drop out. She never achieved full success at anything.

This process we've just completed is useful for information gathering. By using this contrastive analysis procedure, you can pinpoint the precise place where the change work needs to be applied. This can save you time and frustration when you're working with others.

4

Re-Imprinting

 Tim and Suzi were once working with a man who had a fear of flying on airplanes. He had tried many things to change his fear, but none of them worked. They had him access the feelings associated with flying and established a kinesthetic anchor by touching his shoulder. (Anchors are stimulus-response processes where some external stimuli gets paired to an internal state or set of representations. An example of a naturally occurring anchor is a special song that triggers you back to some prior experience whenever you hear it. Bandler and Grinder discovered that anchors can also be deliberately set. Internal states can be paired to an external touch, a sound or something the person can see. Once this association has been set, you can then trigger the internal experience at will. If you establish a kinesthetic anchor, you can hold a state stable by maintaining the touch.)

They suggested that the anchored feeling "take him back in time" to other events where he had experienced that same feeling. Then almost immediately he complained of "drawing a blank." They very patiently held the anchor and paced him, stating that the "blank" was actually quite significant and recommended that he relax and concentrate on the blank. As he relaxed they told him a story, a therapeutic metaphor, about a time when they were out walking in the fog one night in their neighborhood searching for a dog. It was so thick they couldn't see ten feet in front of them and even though they couldn't see through it, they intuitively knew where things were located and were able to find what they were looking for.

After approximately ten minutes he began seeing still, slide images, which he stated could not possibly have anything to do with his phobia. The first slide was of an old gentleman holding some flowers. The man had lived next to him when he was a small child. He then saw additional slides which they were able to piece together into a movie about an early childhood experience.

In this case, it was an experience that he had no recollection of at the conscious level, yet it was significant to the phobia as they explored the connections. He had been playing with other little children in a vacant lot behind the older gentleman's house when they discovered an abandoned refrigerator lying on its back. Somehow one of the other little boys had gotten locked inside and could not get out. The man Tim and Suzi were working with had actually switched positions in his mind with the trapped little boy and was feeling the other child's panic. The children were able to get help and the trapped little boy was rescued before anything serious happened to him.

When the man's father came upon the scene he said, "Let that be a lesson to you. *Never* get into any place that you can't get out of." As an adult, this man got the feeling of panic whenever he was "trapped" on an airplane.

Once they had gotten beyond the "blank" or impasse, they were able to use the re-imprinting process outlined in this chapter to give him new choices about his feeling concerning flying on airplanes. He now reports that he flies on airplanes three or four times a month as a part of his work and is so comfortable that he often sleeps during the flight.

How Imprints Occur And What They Are

An imprint is a significant event from the past in which you formed a belief, or a cluster of beliefs. Every form of healing, whether physical or psychological, that I know of gives credence to the fact that present behaviors are often created or shaped by past behaviors and past events. What's important to us as NLP practitioners about past experiences is *not* the content of what happened, but the impression or belief that the person built from the experience.

The notion of imprinting comes from Konrad Lorenz, who studied the behavior of ducklings when they hatched. He discovered that baby ducks would imprint a mother figure in the first day or so of life. They did that by sorting for movement, so that if something moved just after they hatched from their eggs, they followed it and it "became" their mother. Lorenz would move, and the ducks would follow. He found that if he reintroduced them to their real mother later, they would ignore her and continue to follow him. In the morning, when he got up, he would go outside and find the ducklings curled up around his boots, instead of in their own nest.

He once reported that a ping pong ball rolled by one of the eggs when it hatched and the emerging duckling imprinted to the ping pong ball, making it the "mother." Later in life, the duck would shun others of its own species at mating time and try to mount various kinds of round things.

Konrad Lorenz and his colleagues believed that imprints were established at certain neurologically critical periods, and that once the critical period had passed whatever had been "imprinted" was permanent and not subject to change.

Timothy Leary investigated the imprint phenomena in human beings. He contended that the human nervous system was more sophisticated than that of ducklings and other animals. He established that under the proper conditions, content that had been imprinted at earlier critical periods could be accessed and reprogrammed or re-imprinted.

Leary also identified several significant developmental critical periods in human beings. Imprints established during these periods established core beliefs that shaped the personality and intelligence of the individual. The primary critical periods involved the establishment of imprints determining beliefs about biological survival, emotional attachments and well-being, intellectual dexterity, social role, aesthetic appreciation, and "meta cognition," or the awareness of one's own thought processes. Thus, health problems might stem back to core beliefs and supporting behaviors established during the biological survival critical period, while phobias could have their roots in the emotional well-being period. Learning handicaps might derive from imprints formed during the critical period involving intellectual dexterity, and so on.

My development of the NLP Re-imprinting technique grew out of a series of seminars I co-conducted with Leary. It was as a result of my work with him that I realized that some traumatic episodes experienced by clients were more than just bad memories that could be dealt with by using simple integration techniques. They were often belief and identity forming imprints that formed the cornerstones of a person's personality, and thus they required a different approach in order to influence the person in an adequate and lasting way.

Imprints can be significant "positive" experiences that lead to useful beliefs, or they can be traumatic, or problematic experiences that lead to limiting beliefs. Typically, but not always, they involve the unconscious role modeling of significant others.

Compare the duck's behavior with human behavior using child abuse as a point of comparison. Research validates that often people who have been abused as children unconsciously get into relationships, as adults, that repeat their childhood experience. For example, often women who have been abused as children marry men who abuse them as adults. Males who were beaten as a child may abuse their own children. If they were beaten by their mothers, they may get into relationships where they are somehow the lesser person. Research shows that women who were beaten by their mothers are apt to be more violent with their own children than those who weren't. Imprints are one explanation of this phenomena. People abused as children can imprint that this is the typical behavior associated with fathers, mothers, husbands or wives.

At the time the ducklings were hatching out of the eggs they didn't say, "Gee, that's a strange looking mother; I'd better check things out." Their brains were probably saying, "This is how mothers are,"—human beings do the *same* sorts of things.

Modeling And Taking On The Other's Point Of View

I was once working with a lady who had cancer of the throat. She felt like her throat, and in fact, the rest of her body, wasn't hers. She had the feeling that someone had taken it away from her. I anchored that feeling and had her use the feeling to help her remember an experience in her past. It was a very early childhood memory. She said, "My mother is grabbing me and she's shaking me by the throat." While she was saying this, however, she was making the shaking movement with her own hands. The voice she used was one of anger, like her mother's must have been, not one of a fearful small child. She had switched positions with her mother. She was not exhibiting the behavior of the little child, but the behavior of her mother, the aggressor.

When you're a child, you're in an intense ongoing relationship with your parents. You will imprint (introject) some of their beliefs and behavior and make it part of your own. As one lady put it to me, "When I was little and was beaten by my mom, I just felt hurt and confused. Now that I'm older, I find it easier to identify with the feelings of my mother. Instead of the hurt, scared feelings I got as a child, I get the angry feelings of my mother." Another woman told me that "at times I feel possessed by my mother." As you grow up and your body changes, you typically find it easier to match the behavior of the adult person.

An imprint is not necessarily logical. It's something that's intuitive, and it typically happens at critical developmental periods.

In childhood most of us don't have a real sense of self identity, so we pretend we're somebody else, and we often take on the role model—lock, stock and barrel. We can end up like the ducklings that weren't very discriminating about what they would accept as a mother.

Who you are as an adult is, in many ways, an incorporation of the adult models you've grown up with. Your model of being an adult has the features of past significant others; features that have been stuck in early ways of believing and behaving that you made a part of yourself at an early age. These beliefs and behaviors emerge when you reach a certain age and are not a child anymore. That's why it's as important to deal with the other persons involved as well as the younger you in the Re-imprinting process.

I worked with a woman who wanted to exercise more and really get her body in shape. When we got close to the change she wanted, she had a *really* strong reaction. I asked, "What stops you?" and she said, "If I made this change, then

I'd *really like* myself." That didn't sound so terrible to me, so I asked her how that would be a problem. She replied, "Because if I like myself, then I lose people I care about." I asked her where *that* came from, because that's a belief. "If I like myself and take care of myself, then I lose other people."

It turned out that there was precedence in her family history. When significant others in her family had really done something good for themselves, their partner felt threatened and couldn't handle it. Then the relationship would break up. When my client looked into her future, she got a bad feeling about doing something good for herself. That feeling related to something in other people's pasts. It was role modeled from somebody else. So you can have strong limiting feelings resulting from imagining what it would be like to be in another person's shoes.

Identifying And Working With Imprints

The hardest part of changing any belief system is the fact that the imprint is likely to be out of conscious awareness. Your most significant behaviors are usually the ones that are most habitual. Those are the behaviors that you're least consciously aware of. When using an anchored feeling as a guide to past memories the experiences you remember first may not be as important as going back to the point where you feel confused and say "I don't know." "I don't know why I do that." At that point, you know you're really onto something significant—I often call that an impasse. That's a rather interesting orientation, and is perhaps a different approach than what you might have taken some time in the past. That's when you know you're "at the right address" in terms of identifying the circumstances in which you created the limiting belief.

Drawing A Blank—Impasses

If you're not having any luck finding an imprint associated with an impasse, have the person make up something that might be associated with it. You can say, "Guess what that feeling is all about." That will get you started. If the episode they make up carries the same intensity in their physiology as the problem state, you know there's a connection.

Occasionally when you anchor a feeling, even an intense one, and hold it to assist the person in remembering past experiences, the person will come upon a blank, as did the man with the airplane phobia. Suddenly, there's nothing there to work with. It would appear that some people have learned to dissociate from the pain to avoid what might be coming next. You can anchor that "blank" or dissociated state and take it back in time, on a search for a significant past imprint. You need to be patient with this and often your patience will pay off. The person will often begin to get slide pictures that they can piece together to find the details of the imprint situation.

Another useful technique for identifying imprints, when a person reaches an impasse, is to immediately interrupt them and then anchor a powerful resource state. You might want that resource to be something like courage or power—a generic resource that would be useful in many different situations. Then, take that resource anchor back into the impasse to help the person get through it.

I often find therapeutic stories (metaphors) useful when working towards integration. If you hit an impasse where the conscious mind is doing one thing and the unconscious another, it's useful to tell a metaphor, especially if the person is saying, "It just doesn't make any sense." I have a quote on my wall from Albert Einstein that reads, "Everything should be made as simple as possible, but not simpler." I often tell that to people when they are stuck and suggest that if they try to make something happen faster or less simple than is possible, they sometimes run into resistance. One of the nice things about metaphors is that they're processed by both brain hemispheres, so they bridge thinking gaps nicely. Even if the metaphor is doing no more than repeating what you just said by restating it in an analogy or story, it can be understood at a different level.

Change History Without Role Models

You may occasionally find imprint experiences where there is no obvious introjection of a significant other. Let me give you some examples of imprints where there is not a clear switching of positions with a role model. I worked with a 35 year old man who was a successful executive, but he couldn't spell. We tried to teach him the spelling strategy and he just kept blowing it. It turned out that as soon as he'd look up and left to visualize the spelling word, he'd start associating into an experience where he'd see his teacher's face, looking at him and telling him how bad he was. Then he'd feel bad. The picture was "clogging up" the channels so he couldn't see words, just the teacher's face. He said when he tried to visualize words they wouldn't stay up there in visual memory; they just kept disappearing. His problem stemmed from his relationship to a significant other even though he did not switch position with her.

We explored the positive intention behind his third grade teacher's behavior by having him switch positions with her. He discovered that she was trying to motivate him to learn to spell. Determining the positive intention changed the relationship in his mind and the teacher's face didn't need to hang up there. After that he didn't even have to look back at the word; the letters literally jumped up in his mind. He already had the letters and he knew how to spell words; he just couldn't get access to the words in his mind's eye because of this interference. When we took away the interference (the image of the teacher's face), the words were suddenly there. This is an example of an imprint experience that prevented a person from doing a simple process and resulted in the man's belief that he couldn't spell.

Not long ago, I was called in to work with a professional diver who was afraid of diving in murky water. He had no idea why he was afraid. As he was talking to me about his present state, I noticed that he looked up and left. It was clearly a picture that he was making that was outside of his conscious awareness. Even though he was accessing visually, he said that the water *felt* "squishy." When I asked him what he was aware of visually, he said, "I don't know, I don't see anything." (Often in pinpointing beliefs the person has only a partial awareness of his own thinking process.) I asked him to look up, and exaggerate the feeling, making it stronger, to see if any pictures came to mind. Suddenly, as he began to exaggerate the feeling, a remembered image popped up of when he was playing in a muddy river at the age of 12. They were dredging the river for a body and he stepped on it. That was what bothered him about murky water. Just knowing about that past imprint didn't change the fear. We had to consider what abilities, information or other resources needed to be added to that early experience to make it different.

Since no obvious switching with others was involved, rather than doing a full Re-imprinting, I only needed to do basic anchoring. I had him go back to the experience, and, using basic anchoring techniques, add more choices to give him the desired state. It was a simple step but it made all the difference—he was able to dive in murky water, using *appropriate* caution.

Imprint Experiences with Role Models

An imprint experience generally involves the unconscious role modeling of significant others. The purpose of Re-imprinting is to give you new choices in the way you think about the old imprint experience. These choices assist you in changing the beliefs you made about yourself, the world and the role models.

To accomplish the Re-imprinting, you need to add the resources you would have needed at the time of the experience in order to have had more choices about your behavior. You will probably need to add resources to the other people who were involved in those early experiences also. (See Re-imprinting Process Summary, Steps III and IV, page 96.)

Editor's Note: What follows is a complete transcript of a re-imprinting session with a client, showing how resources are added into the role model, as well as to the client. Note Robert's consistent use of backtrack pacing for rapport and understanding. His comments to the group are also metaphors and explanations for Bill.

Re-imprinting Demonstration

Robert: Bill, why don't you introduce yourself, and tell us what your outcome is for being here today.

(*To Group:*) Bill says he doesn't mind sharing content if it is necessary or appropriate. I use content in several ways. Sometimes it is useful to get *some* content about the significant experiences (imprints) a person has had so you can see how things fit together. I also need enough content to calibrate to the voice tone, accessing cues, physiology, etc. that are associated with Bill's experience. When I ask someone to tell me about "x" experience, I am not concerned with the verbal, conscious answer they're giving. Rather, I'm checking for the body posture, accessing cues, tone and tempo of voice, gestures, and language patterns they adopt. I'll let you know as we go along what information I get from these cues.

Bill: My name is Bill and I'm from San Francisco. Last Fall I was diagnosed as having what's called an AIDS Related Condition, which is a precursor to AIDS. Right now my symptoms are trivial but when taken in totality, the symptoms tell my doctor that my immune system is dicey. I also had a positive test for the AIDS virus.

Robert: I'd like to discuss with you your idea of what a desired state would be.

Bill: Staying alive.

Robert: OK. So staying alive. Now let's get something for your brain to hone in on. Staying alive is a big valuable chunk.

(*To Group:*) I sometimes think of my role at this stage in the work as being a behavioral travel agent. Someone comes into you as a travel agent and you ask, "Where would you like to go?" If they say, "I want to go home," you need a lot more information before you can assist them.

(*To Bill:*) When you think about that, I noticed that your eyes went up. Do you have a picture?

Bill: Sure. I can see myself in the future feeling good and having no symptoms.

Robert: You have a dissociated image. The "no symptoms" statement is a negative statement about what you *won't* have. If you have no symptoms, what will you be like?

Bill: I'm looking healthy.

Robert: What things will you be doing in the healthy future that you aren't doing now?

Bill: I would physically feel better.

Robert: Do you get that "better feeling" when you look at the image?

Bill: If I look at it long enough.

Robert: Long enough?

Bill: I look at myself working out at the gym and feel better.

Robert: Good. How would you expand that to other

contexts as well? Would you be doing anything differently in your relationships or at work?

Bill: I would be spending a lot more time with people. Recently I haven't felt good enough to have a lot of relationships.

Robert: So you'd be spending a lot more time with people.

Bill: Enjoying myself with them.

Robert: Are there any specific people? I don't need specific names.

Bill: Yes. Friends and people at work.

(*To Group:*) Notice that we have an expanded image now. He just started off with an image of looking healthy in a gym. We want him to look at the broader life around that. So we might begin to ask, if you are healthy in *that* setting, what does it mean about the rest of your life?

We need to check for any ecological issues in other life areas that might need to be dealt with. Sometimes health means to the person that they'd really be living life the way they'd really like. When you work with people that want to give up something, they may say, "If I quit smoking, then I'm going to finally be able to do everything that I've always wanted in life." Of course, this means that there are more issues than just quitting smoking, because there is a big implication behind quitting. Health for Bill means a lot more than working out in a gym.

(*To Bill:*) What needs to change inside your body to give you the healthy future you want? Picture the inside of your body right now, and also picture how you would be different as a person if you were the healthy you. Compare the pictures.

Bill: My immune system would be stronger.

Robert: How specifically? What would that look like?

Bill: I don't know. I go to the Simonton model—little Pac Men.[1]

Robert: The Pac Man model of the immune system.

(*To Group:*) The first thing Bill says is that he's never pictured that before. He is saying, "I don't know what that would look like." He jumps to a model that his Pac Men (immune system) would be stronger than the virus, or something like that.

What is AIDS, and what does it do? It is a virus that presents a paradox. It actually attacks certain cells of your immune system. If you try to attack those cells using visualization, you're actually going after your own internal defense system. The AIDS virus infects your immune system's marker cells—the ones that identify what is good in your body versus what the other immune cells need to eliminate. That's why you are more susceptible to infections when you have the AIDS virus. It isn't because you have less Pac Men. The Pac Men aren't infected. The cells that turn the joystick are. What is problematic is that you have to get rid of some of your own immune cells in order to build up your immune system.

So, it's not a matter of having more Pac Men. It's a matter of having them doing the right things. It's not a matter of having the Pac Men eat something, it's a matter of maintaining the integrity of your physical identity. There are lots of examples of people that have the AIDS virus but don't have any of the symptoms. They may never have symptoms, or it can take years for symptoms to develop.

(*To Bill:*) In order to get to the healthy future you want, some things have to be accomplished inside your immune system as well. That's the reason I'm asking what your image is and going into this explanation.

Bill: I understand.

Robert: Your immune system determines what *is self* and what *isn't self.* It's about identity. Sometimes immune system problems and illnesses will correspond to other identity issues as well. That's another reason why I've been asking, "Who are you going to be in your healthy future?"

Let me give you a quick example. People who have

multiple personalities often have different immune reactions in each personality. For instance, they may have an allergy in one personality and not in the other. One woman I read about even had diabetes in one personality and not in the other. One type of diabetes is related to a malfunction where the immune system attacks the cells in your pancreas that produce insulin. By changing your identity you frequently change a whole bunch of other things (such as the immune system), all the way down.

(*To Bill:*) What kind of a picture do you have right now? I've been giving some information that may help you form a present state image.

Bill: I'm seeing a picture of my immune system, but it looks like my circulatory system with the blood vessels collapsed and constricted. The obvious solution is for them to dilate. This looks a lot more realistic to me than the Pac Man image I had before.

Robert: OK. So you want to see something opening up. What is making it collapse and constrict?

Bill: I am.

Robert: How?

Bill: I don't know, but somehow in my mind, I am.

Robert: What would you be doing this to your immune system for?

Bill: I have several guesses. I've used illness in the past to get love. I did that when I had asthma as a kid. I could get attention by being sick. I'm getting attention right now in my life.

Robert: You say, "I notice I'm getting positive gain from this now. Attention."

(*To Group:*) He's also saying, "asthma and constriction." There is some correlation there. We could deal with strategies for getting attention, but I want to deal with underlying beliefs. That will really make the difference.

(*To Bill:*) Do you believe you can do what you need to do to achieve the healthy future you want?

Bill: I'm trying to. My whole experience of NLP for the past two years is that NLP doesn't work for me. I've seen it work over and over on others. I've even used it with other people successfully—but nothing seems to work on me.

(*To Group:*) This is a good indicator that a belief limitation is present. When NLP practitioners ask, "How do you identify a belief?" I often suggest they find something a person has tried to change for a long time but keeps failing to achieve. When Bill talks about what he wants, he looks up and to his right. When he talks about what stops him, he makes a gesture like this (pushes his hand down and to his left behind him). We want to watch for what he does when he says "yes" versus when he says "no." We don't want to interpret it yet, just notice it.

(*To Bill:*) In spite of saying you don't believe you can change, you're still up here in front of the group. At some level you still believe it's possible to get the changes you want.

Bill: I believe it's possible for me to change, I just haven't figured out how to, yet. That's the "cannot."

Robert: When you think about yourself now in comparison with where you want to be, what is in the way?

Bill: Right now I don't get results in the change work I try to do on myself.

Robert: So, it's *just* the fact that you haven't gotten results?

Bill: It's a hideous "Catch 22."

Robert: Let's explore this a little bit. Think of some things you've done. Has there been a time when you thought you would get results?

Bill: I keep thinking I will, but I don't.

Robert: So, you *think* you'll get results.

Bill: Hope. I hope I'll get results, but I don't *think* I will. That's different.

Robert: You say, "I hope I am going to get results." That's different than thinking you will and it's different than *believing* you will. You hope you are, but . . .

Bill: I *don't* know.

(*To Group:*) He said, "I *don't* know." He didn't say "I don't *know*," which is something to consider. When you're going for an outcome, don't just take any piece of information you first get and run with it. What you are after is a *pattern*. That's what NLP is all about—finding patterns in behavior. One of the ways I know I have a pattern is if I have three examples of the same nonverbal cue. When I see or hear the same response, I start to know there is a pattern. If I contrast the physiology three times when someone has failed versus three times when they've succeeded and I see or hear the same things going on, I know I have a pattern.

Another way I know I have discovered a pattern is to see behavioral consistencies around the same category of internal events. This is another way you find an answer when somebody says, "I don't know what stops me" when you are gathering information using the well-formedness conditions for outcomes.

(*To Bill:*) When you first started NLP, did you have a belief that it would work easily on you or did you believe that it wouldn't work?

Bill: When I first started, I had heard some wonderful things about it. I think I had the belief it would work.

Robert: Let's go all the way back to the first time. What's the first thing you tried it with?

Bill: Lower back pain. I worked with an NLP trainer. The work he did alleviated the pain for about an hour.

Robert: So, something happened and it started hurting again. What made it start hurting?

Bill: (Drops voice to auditory tonality.) I don't know what made it start hurting again.

Robert: Right now you were just looking down and to your left, which usually means you are thinking in words. Were you just repeating the question or . . .

Bill: No, I was only aware of feeling my back.

Robert: When you were feeling your lower back your eyes went down and left. Move your eyes down and left. What did the NLP trainer do?

Bill: (Again looks down to the left) A Behavior Generator, where you watch yourself do a new behavior in a situation then step into it and experience it; but it didn't work. I have my own internal terrorist.

Robert: You said you had an internal terrorist. When did you first notice it?

Bill: I'm not sure when I first noticed it. It's always been very difficult for me to get what I want.

Robert: He says, "It's *always been difficult to get what I want.*" That's an example of a belief statement.

Bill: Yes, and it's had an awful effect on my life.

Robert: Where does that belief come from? Do you want to have that belief?

Bill: No.

Robert: How come you still have it then?

Bill: (Frustrated) Because the work I did to change the belief didn't work.

Robert: So, right now, you looked up to your left. (Gestures) What was going on? This time your eyes went way up there. (Gestures up and to Bill's left.)

Bill: I was starting to get angry.

Robert: At what? Put your eyes back up there.

Bill: I'm angry at how difficult my life has been.

Robert: So, what do you see in your mind's eye?

Bill: All sorts of examples of how my life has been difficult.

Robert: How far back do they go?

Bill: Puberty.

Robert: Stay up there for a moment. You said you started feeling angry.

Bill: Yes—angry and frustrated.

Robert: Angry about your life. When you see those examples, that makes you angry.

Bill: No. Frustrated about my life and that makes me angry.

Robert: You say frustration first, and then anger. Usually frustration occurs when you know what the goal is, but you don't know how to get there. So, there have been things you've wanted to do but couldn't. (Bill is nodding.) Have you been frustrated with yourself or the world?

Bill: Myself first.

Robert: Yourself first. I want you to make that image again and take that sense of frustration . . .

(*To Group:*) Notice. Here is a person who needs to have a belief to drive him forward to get healthy. To do all the things it takes to get better may be difficult, sometimes arduous, and sometimes complex. What Bill is saying is that he has many, many examples of failures of getting what he wants. As soon as he gets started trying to make a change, he gets frustrated. All these old memories and behaviors come to mind and interfere with his attempt to get what he wants. Remember, in order to get any goal, you need three things. You need to *want to* get it, *know how to* get it, and *give yourself the chance to* get it. If you have a belief that things will be hard to get for yourself, it will be difficult to give yourself the chance to—to go through all you need to do and hang in there long enough to get what you want. Sometimes hanging in there is what you need to do, even in the face of frustration.

(*To Bill:*) Let's start with the frustration and anger since those emotions seem to be the ones that come out first. You mentioned that it started at puberty. Take a moment and think about how frustrating everything has been. (Anchors the feeling.) Take that feeling back in time—maybe there are words also. (Long pause while Bill remembers)

Robert: What do you see?

Bill: I'd rather not reveal the content.

Robert: That's OK. Does it involve someone else?

Bill: Yes.

Robert: One person, primarily?

Bill: Yes, um hm.

Robert: Do you see that person looking right at you?

Bill: No, I see me and the other person.

Robert: Put yourself inside "the you back then" for just a moment. What generalizations are you making about what is going on?

Bill: How bad I am. (Long pause) That I can't get what I want. That I don't deserve what I want.

Robert: That you don't deserve what you want.

Bill: Also that if I get what I want, it'll get me in a lot of trouble. (Voice shaky, tears and sniffles.)

Robert: Do you have any beliefs you're building about the other person or the world around you?

Bill: The world around me would get on my case if they knew what I wanted. It has to do with gaining cultural acceptance and that sort of thing.

Robert: It has to do with cultural acceptance—what's the intention? The intention behind the thought that the world will get you, even if it only *knows* what you want?

Bill: I don't know. (Voice shaky and emotional)

(*To Group*:) I was trying to find out if there were any generalizations or beliefs about the intent.

(*To Bill*:) (Shifts voice) Now it's time to come out of that. Back here to this room. Robert here (Gestures to self) and Bill here (Gestures to Bill—laughs).

OK. This is the next thing I'd like you to do. Look back at that experience you had during puberty. Put it way out there so it's completely removed—so you're not into it at all. (Gestures out in front of Bill) That's right . . . watch that boy and whoever else is involved, out there, as you are sitting here comfortably.

Bill: (Long pause) I can see it. (Flat voice tone that is associated with watching yourself.)

Robert: How has that experience affected you since that time?

Bill: It's given me a lot of guilt. (Looks up to his left.)

Robert: So you can see that it's given you a lot of guilt. What belief would you have formed about that?

Bill: That what I want is wrong—is bad.

(*To Group:*) That's a little different from what he said earlier. Before he said, I *can't* get what I want. I don't *deserve* to get what I want and if I *do* get what I want, I'll be punished by the world. If the world *knows* what I want, it will punish me anyway. And now what he's saying is, "What I *want* is bad." That becomes an underlying belief. That's a nice little cluster of beliefs that explains why he might have had trouble getting the things he wants.

Let me point something out. Beliefs tend to fulfill themselves. When you try to argue with a belief in the present, the person is confronting all the data, gathered over time, that supports or "proves" their initial belief. When you go back to where it started, often the issues are much simpler and clearer. They're certainly not cluttered by later confirmations. I don't care so much about what happened in the initial puberty experience as I care about how that affected your belief system. At puberty especially, you build a lot of beliefs about yourself, your identity, and your sexuality.

Remember, we had Bill look back to see if there were any other beliefs or other ways that this experience had affected him. I have a reason for doing that. We had him first go back inside the imprint and experience it again to get some physiology for us to see and hear. I asked "What kind of beliefs are you building there?" so that I could identify a pattern in his voice tone. Sometimes when you have the person put the belief into words, it's the first time they've verbalized it. By doing this, we are beginning to involve a bit more of the brain in the whole process, which can then help us find a solution.

The reason I have the person look back on the reference experience afterwards is that sometimes the experience was confusing or actually positive at the time it occurred. Let's take a confusing example of when someone was sexually molested by a parent. Often they were little and may not have known what to think about the situation. They might not have formed a belief at that time—they were just doing what Mommy or Daddy or Uncle Ernie wanted. It's only *later* that they build a belief like, "I've been soiled for life." The point is that there might be beliefs that you build both during and after an imprint experience.

(*To Bill:*) There was also a significant other person involved.

Bill: There was also more than one specific experience. There were a series of experiences within a time span. (Gestures out to left)

Robert: (Repeats gesture) A time span. Good, we want to know where that is. Bill, what I want to do now is a process called Re-imprinting.

(*To Group:*) Let me review what we've done. There was a certain frustration associated with Bill's belief that he could change, and we took that back in time. We aren't concerned with the content of the experience; we're concerned with the generalizations—the beliefs—that got formed.

Imprints may be single experiences, or a series of experiences that happen over and over. So, a person believes that's the way reality is. There's a question that I want to ask Bill in reference to his group of experiences.

(*To Bill:*) Did the belief that you were wrong only come from your experiences and what you felt was going on? Or was it formed by judgments that were passed by the significant other person?

Bill: Judgments by the other person and myself as well, at later dates.

Robert: And yourself at later dates, too. One of the things you find with imprints is that the beliefs of significant other people are *as important* in the creation of your beliefs as your own experience is. When you are in puberty, it's not hard to temporarily reject that significant other person's views. But sometimes as you grow older, and acquire an adult belief system, the significant other's beliefs begin to take on more power.

I'd like you to review the movie of your experience at puberty, and watch both yourself and the significant other person. My guess is, Bill, when you talk about an unconscious internal terrorist, you're talking about the fact that your brain runs some aspect of the significant other's behavior over and over again. But this time you're experiencing it as *you*, not as the significant other. I'm wondering what resource the other person needed. I take it that this other person was participating in the judgments that you have about yourself.

Bill: That other person is where I *got* the judgments I have about myself.

Robert: Is that person trying to install a belief in you that you don't deserve what you want? Is that the intention?

Bill: No. He is trying to install other beliefs in me. He's trying to install a belief in me that a certain category of behavior is bad. All my other beliefs come from that.

Robert: What is his intention in doing that? Is his *intention* to screw you up?

Bill: No, it's to take care of me.

Robert: To take care of you. If he were to know now what's going on with you, would he be satisfied?

Bill: No, he wouldn't want me to feel badly about myself.

Robert: What would you need to give that person in order for him to respond differently?

Bill: (Searches his mind) More acceptance.

Robert: So he needs a realization that different people have different models of the world. To be more accepting of others. Bill, have *you* ever had the kind of feeling you're talking about—being more accepting? About anyone or anything?

Bill: Yes.

(*To Group:*) I'm asking *Bill* if he's ever had the resource this significant other needed.

(*To Bill:*) I want you to vividly remember a time when *you* fully had that accepting feeling. Find a specific experience.

Bill: (Long pause—nods.) I have had that specific feeling of acceptance.

Robert: (Anchors resource state) Take this feeling and give it to this other person. This other person is in your brain right now—that image, that memory is coming from your brain. Take this (Squeezes anchor) and give it to him. What does he do differently?

Bill: That . . . it doesn't matter what I do. He still loves me.

Robert: How does he look at you when he says that? How does he say it? How does that younger boy respond?

Bill: He feels wonderful.

Robert: What beliefs does he build there?

Bill: Um . . . that I'm OK. I don't need to feel guilty for what I want. That it's OK to be me.

Robert: (Firmly) *That it's OK to be me.* Run that same feeling through that whole time period. If that same feeling had been there that whole time . . . how would things have developed differently? You don't have to say anything out loud. Just do it inside, and allow your unconscious mind to review each experience with this belief and feeling. (Squeezes anchor.) We know that this person didn't have the resource of acceptance at the time, although it's a resource that *you* have. You *can* treat yourself that way. You can update that model now, so that you know with that new resource, you don't have to keep replaying frustration over and over.

Now, Bill, there is a younger self back in that experience that also needs resources he didn't have then. If you look back at him now, is that the belief you want to build from your experience? Look at all these beliefs—I don't deserve it, I'm bad, etc. I'm not sure those are the beliefs you want to build as a result of that experience. What would that younger you have needed? What resources do you have *now* that would have allowed you to build a different set of beliefs at puberty?

Looking back on that experience now, what sort of belief would you rather have built?

Bill: Um . . . That I can accept myself no matter what kind of feedback I'm getting.

Robert: OK. So you can accept yourself no matter what kind of feedback you're getting from the outside world. It seems to me that if you had known that the judgments of others are *their* models of the world and not yours, the experience would have meant something else. When you look back on that other person's views, was he *right?* By the way, he wasn't even accomplishing what he wanted. He didn't want you to build limiting beliefs, either. He behaved the way he did through his own beliefs and belief system. It's useful to recognize that others have their own models. Their models don't have to impact you.

Bill: The other person was well intentioned, but was off base.

Robert: I don't think you knew that when you were a child, having that experience.

Bill: I didn't. I thought he was right.

Robert: You thought he was right. It makes a lot more sense to say, "He's well intentioned but off base." That's something you know now. You said you wanted to know you were OK no matter what kind of feedback you received. Have you had that experience since that time? Even if it was only for a glimmer?

Bill: Oh, sure.

Robert: Think of a time when you knew you were OK. You felt OK no matter what feedback you got.

Bill: I lied. No, I don't have a time.

Robert: What is the closest you've come to having that resource? One of the nice things about anchoring and submodalities is that we can build the resource you need.

Bill: (Remembers a time.)

Robert: (Anchors Bill as his physiology shifts.) What was going on there?

Bill: Someone was angry with me on the telephone, being rude, but I knew what he was saying wasn't what was really happening.

Robert: OK. How did you know that? What let you know that inside? (Touches anchor.)

Bill: A feeling I had, right here. (Points to heart area.)

Robert: (Touches anchor.) Can you emphasize *that* feeling? That's a good feeling to have, too. If you made a picture of it, what would it look like? What would it sound like?

Bill: It would look like a circular light.

Robert: What if you made that light brighter?

Bill: It feels better.

Robert: What if you make it bigger, so it surrounds more of you?

Bill: I start going into a smile.

Robert: Yeah . . . Now what I'd like you to do is to take that light (Touches anchor) and shine it back in your history. Shine it on that younger you. (Robert's voice tempo is matching Bill's breathing) Make the light shine from that place in you (where Bill had touched his heart) to the same place in him . . . so that even though that other person is saying those things that he said, that younger you is in touch with this light, and it can grow bigger and brighter in him. . . . I'm wondering how he would have responded differently to that other person. Would he have talked to him in a different way? Would the younger you have said, "I think you're well intentioned, but you're off base?"

Bill: No. The younger me just would have let him say what he wanted to say but wouldn't have been affected by it.

Robert: How would that have affected the other person?

Bill: He wasn't really paying a lot of attention to what was going on with me anyway. I'm not sure it would have affected him one way or the other.

Robert: Maybe you would have liked to get attention from him.

Bill: Sure I would.

Robert: If you had *that* (Squeezes anchor) would you have gotten the attention you needed, or would you have needed something else, also?

Bill: It was very difficult to get positive attention from him.

Robert: Then I'm going to ask you to do this. It seems to me that another resource is needed here, both in terms of the imprint experience and also in terms of what is going on with your illness. You said earlier that unless you were sick you couldn't get positive attention. I'm wondering if there has been a time since you had that experience when you've been able to get positive attention from somebody?

Bill: Yes.

Robert: What are those resources? Think of a specific time.

Bill: When I'm just being relaxed and being myself. It's a feeling of being at ease with people. (Bill's physiology shifts into a state of being "at ease." Robert anchors resource state on Bill's shoulder.)

Robert: We'll take this too (Touches that resource anchor which is on Bill's upper arm), and take both of these back to that younger you. . . . That is a little different, isn't it?

Bill: Well, that makes getting attention from him like a challenging game.

Robert: Um hm. And what does he do? (Bill smiles) Let's take these two resources (Touches both anchors) and shine the light over all those experiences back there and brighten them up. Take this resource (Touches anchor) of acceptance back too. Make sure these resources are appropriate for all those experiences. Let the light shine through like a beam, connecting all those experiences together . . .

(Robert's voice shifts to a soft hypnotic tone and tempo.) You can be relaxed and secure, being calm and comfortable with yourself. Make it into a fun challenge to get what you want.

Bill: Yes!

Robert: We have one more important thing to do. You reviewed this in a dissociated way by *watching* yourself. I'd like to go back and have you put yourself into the experience. Remember, I had you give necessary resources to that significant person. Now, I want you to *go back behind the other person's eyes.* You're going to be in his shoes with *this* resource (Touches anchor as Bill closes his eyes) in those situations. Say what you would say and see what you would see through his eyes. See that young boy in front of you who is building a model of the world, knowing that you can really pay attention to him and give him the support he needs to be accepting of himself, as well as others. And when you're through you can come all the way back here . . . taking all the time you need to finish.

Bill: (Sighs, opens eyes, and looks at Robert.)

Robert: There was that young boy, who needed to know at his core that he was OK, that he could be relaxed and confident and get the attention he needed. You saw how that would have been different if he had the resource associated with the light and also the ability to get attention.

Step into the experience, be him, and take these (Holds all three resource anchors) with you, seeing through his eyes. Have him look up at the other person who now has the resources he needs . . . and run through all the situations. Grow him all the way up to the you that is sitting here. Take with you those new beliefs, those new understandings and spread them through these experiences that in the past have only been evidence of failure. They are now evidence of the new belief. (Robert is matching his voice tempo to Bill's breathing.)

Bill: There is a hole over here (Gestures, in space, by his left ear). The "you're bad" statements are no longer coming at me, but I have a weird "void" feeling.

Robert: What would you like to put in that hole?

Bill: Um . . . that I'm a loving, gentle man just the way I am, and that's fine. If other people want to make judgments about me, that's their problem.

Robert: Put that in there. I want you to *hear that*. Fill up that hole with that sound so it resonates and reverberates back and forth. Say it in as many ways as you can, with as many feelings as you have. So if you're frustrated, or happy or angry or whatever, you know you're just a loving, gentle man and it's just fine. If others are going to make judgments, that's their problem. You always have the choice of getting positive attention from them. Say it louder, make the sound bigger and fill up the hole with sound. OK, now, what was that you wanted when you first sat down? Something about being healthy. Has that image changed?

Bill: I look fuller, more solid in that image.

Robert: Do you deserve that?

Bill: (congruently) Yes!

Robert: Will you take care of yourself in the ways we've discussed?

Bill: Absolutely.

Editor's Note: When Robert's intervention began, Bill's skin color was pale and grey and his posture was slumped down. At the end of the Re-imprinting process, his skin color had changed to a more healthy glow and he was sitting up much straighter.

Questions

Woman: You had Bill watch the whole memory, seeing himself and the significant other person. Then you had him step into both himself and the other person and behave more resourcefully. Will you summarize the process?

Robert: What you've just described is the essence of Re-imprinting. Once you've found the imprint experience, you want to give resources to *both* the person you're working with and any significant others that were present in the imprint experience. Remember, you're not changing the significant other people; the client is changing his own perspective—the belief that he took in as his own as a result of the imprint experience. When you take multiple perspectives on a situation, even without adding resources, you will make it a different experience.

Try this—think of an unpleasant experience you've had with someone else, maybe an argument or when someone said something that hurt your feelings. Remember it as if it were happening right now . . . now float up and look down on the situation, seeing both yourself and the other person. Watch the other person and notice their posture, their voice tone, the way they move and gesture and consider anything you know about *their* experience, both recently and historically. . . . Now float down into them, adopting their physiology as completely as possible. Re-experience the event fully looking from their eyes back at you. . . . When you've re-experienced the event fully from their point of view, float out to the side and watch it over again seeing yourself . . . and the other person. Now step back into yourself as if it was happening all over again. Notice how the experience is different.

Having more information from multiple perspectives will create a change in your own point of view. It's a very powerful set of moves. Having multiple perspectives is the basis for wisdom in decisions, conflicts, negotiations and in cleaning up your own personal history.

Man: Would you give perpetrators, such as rapists, abusers, etc. resources the same way you did with Bill's "significant other"?

Robert: One of the reasons for doing Re-imprinting is to have the client realize what sort of resources people, including abusers and rapists, need in order to completely resolve or avoid the situation. Often when someone has been a victim of a crime, like rape or some other form of violence, they don't want to give the "son of a bitch" resources because that would seem to make the behavior okay. They are really angry about it and have a good reason to be. It would be like forgiving them or excusing the behavior, and they don't want to let go of it or somehow condone the behavior.

Actually, the outcome of giving the perpetrator resources is not to condone their behavior or to make the memory go away. Instead, it is important for the victim to understand what resources the other person would have needed to be the kind of person who would have behaved differently. Often, when a person has been the victim of some kind of crime, their limiting belief maintains itself through anger or fear. Giving the perpetrator resources is a step toward helping them move beyond this. There is no way that you're supposed to make the heinous activity seem okay.

It is a good idea, in most cases, to give the perpetrator the resources they need *prior* to the incident where the imprint experience occurred. Let me give you an example.

I worked with a woman whose mother became enraged and held her out a window that was five stories high. She was so angry she was going to drop her to the street and kill her. To ask this woman what resources her mom needed while hanging her daughter out of the window would have been ridiculous. Instead, I asked the woman to run the movie backwards—back to a time before the incident ever occurred, and I installed the resources there. With the proper resources, the mother would never have "lost it" and threatened her daughter that way. It is similar to working with a phobia. You want the person with whom you are working to start the recollection of the phobic experience *before* the incident occurred, when they were still safe. They then run a dissociated movie, where they watch their younger self all the way through the incident until they were again safe.

You can think of a phobia as a specialized form of an imprint. When working with a phobia, you want to sandwich fear in between times of safety.[2] Consider *that* a general principle in working with any traumatic imprint. Go from resource state (or at least neutral state) to trauma to resource state. That way of working with someone helps to isolate the event and gives it an "ending" for them.

Man: Some imprints are fairly traumatic. Does just leaving the client dissociated as does the fast phobia method make this an incomplete piece of work?

Robert: Often the fast phobia procedure is all that you need to do. Remember, you re-associate them in the last step of the procedure, when you have them re-experience the trauma backwards. Sometimes, however, there is an imprint that needs to be taken care of as well. Freud had a belief that a phobia was an example of displaced anxiety. The person really had fear or some other emotion that was directed toward some significant other person. In order to resolve the phobia, the person's "real" fear had to be uncovered and dealt with first. Of course the problem with that is that people have to go through a lot of pain until the relationship issues are resolved. With NLP we can resolve the feelings right away, so people don't have to keep experiencing fear and panic. Sometimes there is still some other relationship issue or some other imprint behind it that still needs to be worked out.

In many of the traumatic imprints I have worked with

that resulted in phobias, another person *was* involved. I remember working with a lady who had a phobia of moths. This was a lady who could hold a live tarantula in her hand comfortably, but when a little moth flew by she'd freak out. The initiating cause for her phobia was that as a child a little friend had chased her around while holding a bottle containing a big luna moth. She felt humiliated in front of her other friends, but rather than putting the fear and anger onto her friend, she attached her fear to the moth. I did the NLP phobia cure with her and removed the fear, but that alone did not resolve all of the issues she had about that situation.

You might also run into other kinds of phobias that require more than just relieving the panicky feelings. These sometimes come when children were left alone by their parents and something bad happened. One lady I worked with had a fear of water because she nearly drowned. She nearly drowned because she was trying to swim away from her mother who was beating the crap out of her. The phobia technique removed the fear she had about the water, but obviously there were other issues we needed to deal with as well.

Woman: When you have re-imprinted a past trauma, or resolved conflicting identity structures, how do you know whether the person has adequate strategies to continue the change in a positive way? How do you know if the person still has ways of getting what they want?

Robert: Let me respond to that by way of a story. David Gordon (an NLP trainer and author) and I once worked with a lady who had a hand washing compulsion. She thought that these things she called "real imaginary fleas" would get on her. They were "real" in the sense that she would "feel" them when they got on her, but were "imaginary" because she knew that no one else experienced them. She had been cursed with these fleas for fifteen years and had built her life around them.

The fleas directed her life in certain ways. She had seventy-two pairs of gloves that she wore for different situations. She had to avoid some people more that others to avoid getting their fleas. Her parents were particularly infested, so even though she "loved them dearly," she had to limit her contacts with them. Because the fleas were imaginary, they could do things that ordinary fleas could not, like come through the telephone. Because of that, she couldn't talk to her folks on the phone very long.

In working with her, I suggested that we treat her real imaginary allergy to her real imaginary fleas. I told her it was obviously an allergic reaction because even though the fleas were all over other people they weren't affected like she was. It was just that she had an allergy to the fleas like some people have to pollen. This really interrupted her thinking about the fleas. She did not have an automatic belief about a real imaginary allergy, so I gave her some sugar pills, and carefully paced her thinking process, by telling her that these real imaginary pills would cure her allergy.

She came back the next week and was genuinely frightened because the pills had worked. She no longer knew what kind of clothes to buy, because she had always bought clothes that were a couple of sizes too big. That way the sleeves would cover her hands and protect her from the fleas. She no longer knew how to treat her parents, cook food, or go about her other daily activities because the concern for the fleas was no longer there as her life organizing principle.

She needed strategies for all kinds of things. We worked with her on a new decision strategy and had her model other people to gain new behaviors and so forth. The point of this story is that often after you help someone change a limiting belief, their old ways of doing things no longer fit, and you need to offer them new strategies.

One of the most amazing ecology objections you'll get

from people is an interesting one. You get to a certain point in a procedure and they will say,"If I do what you're asking me to do, I really *will* change"! They'll balk at moving an internal image or at completing a visual squash or whatever you're asking them to do. They aren't certain that they are ready to change their identity.

Woman: How important is it that the person think the imprint is a real experience instead of an imagined one?

Robert: I had a woman come to me who had joined a religious order that used meditation and celibacy. She was complaining because when she would try to meditate, she'd see a big penis in her mind, and she couldn't make it go away. It was a real concern for her. Everyone kept telling her what a saint she was, but she thought she was really bad.

Experiences like the one this woman was having are typically communications about something from your unconscious mind. I suggested that we find out what this communication was about. Evidently, there was an imprint about something bad that happened when she was really young. She didn't know what it was and she was afraid of it, so she avoided thinking about it. I suggested she take that fuzzy picture and push it way out there on the wall, just the size of a postage stamp. It was far enough away so that she dissociated from it. She started to look at it and could see that there was a man and woman involved with something sexual—she didn't know what it was. As she kept bringing the picture closer, the issue came up.

She thought she may have been molested by her father when she was a child, but she wasn't sure. She couldn't remember what happened and felt confused. It could have been a story her mother told her (in a convincing voice) about her mother's father, that she pictured, associated with, and got the feelings for, as if it had happened to her. It didn't matter whether it happened to her or her mother, because it was *real* in her experience.

She had never confronted this issue. It was just something big and dark and bad. She invented a number of possibilities that might have occurred. Finally, I told her it didn't really matter. The important thing was that there was some resource that she needed that she didn't have. I had her play each possibility out and pretend it was the "real" one, and find the solution for each one. Here is a person who for 25 years had built a lifestyle on an experience that she didn't even know was objectively real or not. That's why sometimes to a large extent what "really happened" is irrelevant.

Man: After you do re-imprinting, how do you know what really happened?

Robert: You're actually giving people the opportunity to update what they are carrying around inside their head. We're not trying to confuse them about reality; we're allowing them to re-experience the same things without the scar and the negative impact. We end up with different beliefs, different resources and the imprint means something completely different.

We're not trying to erase what actually happened, because the content of the imprint is not what makes the difference anyway. It's what you've *learned* from it and the reminder that you now *have* what you need in terms of resources that's important.

The Re-imprinting Process Summary

I. Identify the specific feelings (it may also be words or an image) associated with the impasse. (Anchor it.) Most people want to avoid these feelings because they are uncomfortable. But it is important to remember that avoiding them won't resolve the limitation. Have the person stay with the feeling (hold your anchor) and remember back to the earliest experience of the feeling associated with the impasse.

A. While the person is still in that associated, regressed state, have him/her verbalize the generalizations or beliefs that were formed from that experience.

II. Dissociate the person from the experience. Have him/her see the experience as if he/she was watching a movie of himself/herself.

B. Ask the person to verbalize any other generalizations or beliefs that were formed as a result of the imprint experience. (Beliefs are often formed "after the fact".)

III. Find the positive intent or secondary gain of the feeling of impasse. Also, if there were significant others involved in the memory, find the positive intention of his/her behavior as well. This may be done by directly asking the people you see in the image.

IV. Identify and anchor the **resources** or choices that the person and the significant others each individually needed then, and did not have then, but **the person does have available now.** Remember that you don't need to limit yourself to the capabilities the person or the significant others had at that time. Just as long as the person (not the significant others) has those resources available now, you may use them to help change that experience.

V. For each of the significant others in the imprint experience, have the person replay the movie, seeing how the experience would have changed if the necessary resources had been available to that person. Do this one at a time for each person making sure the identified resources would be sufficient to change the experience. If not, go back to Steps 3 and 4 and identify other positive intentions or resources that may have been overlooked.

    A. After the resources have been added, ask the person to verbalize what new generalizations or beliefs he/she would choose as a result of adding these resources.

    VI. Utilizing the resource anchors set in Step 4, have the person **relive the imprint experience** from the point of view of each of the significant people involved (one at a time). Have him/her actually step into the other person's body and see the experience out of that person's eyes. Have the person end by stepping into the younger him/her so that he/she experiences it while associated into that younger self. Through this entire process you are holding the resource anchors. Go through the new experience enough times that it is as strong as the original imprint.

    A. Ask the person to update or modify the generalizations he/she would now make from the experience.

VII. Holding the resource anchors utilized throughout the process, have the person come back up through time, from the point of the original imprint to the present. Suggest that as he/she comes back up through time, he/she can think of other occasions in his/her life when these resources that are anchored in now would also have been a useful addition in changing other experiences.

ENDNOTES

1. Carl Simonton and Stephanie Matthews-Simonton, *Getting Well Again* (New York, New York: Bantam Books, 1982). At the Simonton Cancer Counseling Center, patients practice a kind of meditation called imagery in conjunction with traditional cancer treatments. They visualize the cancer cells being overwhelmed by their treatment and flushed out of their bodies.

2. The NLP Phobia Technique is described in *Using Your Brain—For a Change* by Richard Bandler, available through Real People Press, Moab, Utah.

5

Incongruence and Conflicting Beliefs

 We've all had times when we are of two minds about something. Have you ever decided that you'll get up early and exercise, but when morning rolls around you notice how comfortable the bed feels and how sleepy you are? You sleep in and then all day a voice in your mind tells you how bad you are? Or have you unenthusiastically run an errand for a friend when you really wanted to do something for yourself? These are examples of incongruence.

Incongruence is usually experienced as an inner conflict with yourself. Often it seems like there are two sides of yourself. It's like there are two "yous." You have a part of you that wants to do something and a part that objects to it. It could be two behaviors, two beliefs, two belief systems, or even two aspects of your identity.

Sometimes, when you're struggling with belief and identity conflicts, one "part" is not even aware of the other part. The result is confusion about yourself. I remember a woman telling me that she couldn't understand why her husband kept saying she was a critical person. She didn't think of herself that way and had been saying affirmations about being a loving and giving person for six months. The conscious part of her that wanted to reach out to others was out of touch with the part of her that knew she needed to meet her own needs as well. This made her feel defensive and resentful of others when her own needs were neglected. Until these two aspects of herself were integrated so that she could take both her own feelings and the feelings of others into account, she was unhappy and unpredictable in her behavior.

Causes Of Incongruity

Incongruity can result from imprint experiences, modeling significant others, conflicts in hierarchy of criteria, and life transitions and passages.

Imprints

Imprints can and do create internal conflict, as we saw with Bill in the previous chapter. Even after you successfully re-imprint a part of your personal history, you may still have an incongruence to resolve about what beliefs will now characterize the "new you" into the future. Your issue doesn't directly have to do with the past after a Re-imprinting but rather the present and the future.

Modeling

Perhaps at one point in your life, you were raised by someone who held a certain belief that you modeled (like "you must always put others first"), and then something happened that you went on to be raised by someone else with different beliefs (such as "my needs come first") who you also modeled. The beliefs that you modeled and made a part of yourself are internally incompatible.

When you have modeled these opposing beliefs you may feel damned when you look out for yourself or damned when you put others first. Either way you can't be right and are in a double bind.

You could have alternatively modeled different members of your family who had conflicting beliefs. It could be that your Dad smoked and your Mom thought that was bad. If you smoke as an adult, you might replay that conflict in your parent's relationship over and over in your mind, assuming you introjected the conflict in a large chunk way. You pick up the different criteria, values, and strategies for how to think about things from the significant other people in your life that you have modeled.

Hierarchy of Criteria

Conflicts inside us are often conflicts of criteria. You might say "I want the new house with the view, but I need to save my money for retirement." You end up buying the house and then worrying about the future. Unlike conflicts of beliefs, belief systems or aspects of your identity that are dissociated from each other, criteria are arranged as a hierarchy. Criteria will be dealt with more fully in Chapter 6.

Life Transitions and Passages

Life transitions and passages can also create conflict. For example, a man I'll call George worked for the "X" company with his father and uncles. They were staunch union supporters who distrusted the management and held traditional "blue collar values." Much of George's identity had been built by listening to and observing his family's values and behaviors. When he was suddenly promoted to a high paying "white collar" supervisory position, he was confronted with a whole barrage of unpredicted conflicts. He asked himself, "Does this mean I'm different from or better than my father? Do I become a yuppie now and take on new values and discard any old beliefs and values? Do I become one of the people my family and I have always criticized and hated, by virtue of my own success?" This kind of transition created a conflict of beliefs for George, even though in our culture the move would be considered "success" for George.

Life transitions are not just about the details of a change, they're about *who you are* and *what you are*. As I worked with my mother on her health issues back in 1982, when so many things in her life were changing, we discovered that she had a big conflict about being a mother and being an independent person who looked after herself. She would say, "It's very important that I take care of other people, but I now finally have the time to do things just for me. I need a vacation from all this stress." Then she would shift and say, "Maybe I'm being too selfish in thinking about all these things I need for myself." She would flip back and forth between these two belief systems in practically the same sentence with no conscious awareness that she was giving two conflicting messages. I had her visualize each aspect of herself.

One part, the "mother identity," looked like an old hag when she visualized it. It was kind of tired, wanted to rest, but always wanted to take care of other people. It represented one of her missions in life.

The other part was much less developed. It looked like a "jet-setter" that wore bright clothes and didn't look like her. This "jet-setter" part was saying, "Get out of all that mother stuff, with other people relying so heavily on you that you can't even get away and take care of yourself."

These two parts definitely represented different ways of being and they didn't even like each other. These differences showed up as an asymmetry in her body as she talked about her outcome. By "asymmetry" I mean that she gestured with her right hand when talking about her "mother part" and her left hand when she talked about the part that wanted her to do for herself. Her gestures were not together in the movement of both hands.

These conflicts covered all areas of her life, including her will to live. The conflict became so pressing and so pervasive that when she thought of herself as being dead, it seemed peaceful to her.

Both her mother and her sister died of breast cancer. When we discussed the possibility of her getting well, she felt guilty. She'd look back and say, "These were my role models. Who am I to be any better than they were?" I then asked her to not just consider her *own* role models, but to look into the future and to see her daughter (my sister) looking at her to see how *she* should be in life. This had a very powerful impact on her. When she thought about her daughter, she didn't want *her* to get breast cancer just because she had experienced it as a role model. This helped to re-imprint some of my mother's old beliefs in relation to role modeling in this situation.

To summarize, even after you successfully re-imprint a part of your personal history, you may still have incongruence to resolve. Often, you're left with "two sides" of yourself after Re-imprinting. It can either be two beliefs or two aspects of your identity that aren't compatible with each other. It doesn't have to do with the past anymore, it has to do with creating a new present and future identity.

Identifying Conflicts

When you are working with someone who has conflicting beliefs, you will often observe an asymmetry in body posture. It's not as subtle as skin color changes or other minimal physiological cues and is usually quite easy to see. You know you're dealing with two dissociated parts when the person is gesturing with the left hand as she discusses one aspect of the problem and the right hand for the conflicting aspect. It's interesting to note that often the right hand (which relates to the left brain, in most right handed people who have normally organized eye accessing cues) has intentions that deal with relationships and being worthwhile as a person in contexts that involve others. The left hand (which relates to right brain functions) tends to relate more to the individual being her own person and having a rich, full life. This kind of conflict might be defined as the difference between an "other-oriented" part and a "self-oriented" part.

You might also find an "excitatory" and "inhibitory" conflict where you have one part that has great ideas and wants to move ahead while the other part wants you to hold back. This inhibits you from moving ahead. One man I worked with had great ideas for starting his own business but another part wanted him to stay in his current government job because it had "security." He ended up with two separate identities at war with each other. When he thought about leaving his job and starting a business, he'd get anxious. When he stayed on his present job, he'd get depressed.

When working with these kinds of conflicts, you'll get different physiologies associated with each part or belief. The man who wanted to start his own business described his plans in a high fast voice, looked up to his right (visual construct) and gestured with his left hand. When talking about security, he used a slow even voice and his left hand lay still in his lap. One way to know that there is a conflict involved is to watch someone as they are describing an outcome. If you don't see a whole body symmetry in terms of gestures, (both hands moving at the same time in the same way) that's a red flag to alert you to possible conflicting beliefs.

Working With Conflicting Beliefs

The process that many NLP trained people would consider using to deal with two conflicting parts is the visual squash.[1] The typical visual squash where you integrate two behaviors or collapse two anchors won't work when you have two parts that differ dramatically. It doesn't work well if you are associated into either of the two parts and you judge the other part negatively. Let me give you a typical example of this.

One of my clients went through a very hard grief process after unexpectedly losing a close relative. He started overeating and putting on a lot of weight. He had a major conflict between two aspects of his identity.

Historically, he had been a rather chubby child and hadn't felt good about himself. He had felt scared much of the time and the world seemed like an overwhelming place. When he reached puberty, however, he grew to be rather tall and muscular and looked like Tom Selleck and thought he could do anything.

When I worked with him and we began sorting out and identifying each part, it became clear that he had one part that was full of worries, had lots of regressive thoughts, and even got paranoid about nuclear war. On the other hand, he had a part that was very confident and figured he could be successful at whatever he wanted to do. Each part was associated with a different time in his life. The "paranoid" side was almost the complete opposite of the "confident" side. Each was everything the other was not.

I had him dissociate from the parts by fully imagining them—how they looked, sounded, and moved—in his hands. As he described the parts, it became clear that each one was defined only in relation to the other, like matter and anti-matter, or like a communist or anti-communist (one doesn't exist without the other). When he'd identify with the aspect of his identity that "could do anything," he thought of the other part as both weak and useless. When he identified with the part that made him feel paranoid, he said the other part wasn't "real," it was just something he had made up. The identity of one was everything the other was not.

I realized that I couldn't just collapse two anchors or use hypnotic language to squash two pictures together to get an integration because of the beliefs involved. If I had tried and been successful, I'm positive that we would have created a disintegration of his thinking process. I had to very carefully have him sort out the parts by dissociating him from each of them as he imagined them in his hands.

As each part became more fully defined, it became clear that we needed to come up with a new belief system that included both conflicting co-identities. The way we accomplished this was to "out frame" each part's intention (using the question, "What will having that get for you?") until we found *common* intentions for each part. My client was then able to integrate these parts into a new identity, a new self image, which existed at a higher logical level of thinking. As a word of caution, it is really important to find *common intentions* for each aspect of the identity before trying to integrate them. Otherwise, as I said earlier, you could create a disintegration of the person's thinking processes.

Your goal in integrating dissociated aspects of a person's identity is to create a new self image. Referring back to my mother's conflict, when she put those two parts of herself together (the "Mother" and the "jet-setter"), a very interesting image appeared. The image that spontaneously occurred for her was this shimmering, shining, gigantic winged Mercury with wings on his head but who had great big feet that were well grounded.

Belief Conflict Demonstration

Editor's Note

Dee has suffered from asthma and allergies for most of her life. She had an especially severe reactions to cats. Robert had Dee contrast her present state (asthma and allergic reactions to cats) with her desired state—feeling and behaving in a healthy way when exposed to cats. When Robert asked her what stopped her from achieving her outcome of health, she had a feeling which she described as "helpless and worthless" but also had anger associated with it. He anchored this feeling and asked her to let the feeling guide her back in time to discover its origins. She discovered a series of experiences where her parents would fight and argue and ignore her when she was an infant. It's always amazing how you can anchor a familiar adult feeling and use it to guide a client back to pre-verbal experiences. It's usually the easiest and fastest way to achieve age regression to find the origin of problem imprints.

The experiences Dee recalled had to do with lying in her crib while crying and needing attention, but not getting the attention she needed because her parents were arguing with each other. At this point in working with Dee, Robert used the Re-imprinting procedure described in Chapter 4, tailoring it to Dee's specific case.

Often when you have helped the person add the appropriate resources needed to resolve the historical issues that have led to the limiting belief, she will still not have all her resources organized in such a way to reach her desired goal. As has been mentioned, often these resources are organized in separate "parts" or aspects of a person's identity and are not available in an integrated way.

This demonstration begins at the point where Robert is testing the results of the Re-imprinting with Dee and discovers a major conflict.

Robert: Go back to this part down here. (Leads her eyes to the position they were in when she got the helpless feeling during the Re-imprinting.)

Dee: I feel curious and scared.

Robert: About . . .?

Dee: I feel a sense of danger like there's something out there that's kind of scary.

Robert: What is it that's still out there? What is it that you still need?

Dee: What first comes to mind is that I need a guarantee that I won't get hurt, but I think that won't happen. I feel like there's a sense of destruction.

Robert: Is it that "something" would destroy you?

Dee: Yes. It would destroy me.

Robert: Do you know what it is?

Dee: It feels like a black hole.

(*To Group:*) There is a picture here that "feels like a black hole." Notice that Dee is looking down, sort of to her right. Her pupils are dilated and she's describing a *color.* Her eye position indicates feeling and she is also describing a color. This is a synesthesia. Synesthesia is when you are experiencing more than one representational system at the same time. It often makes unpleasant experiences harder for the person to make sense of internally—it's like the experience is less sorted out in her mind. Instead of getting a complete image or sound, it may seem fragmented and hard to decipher from within. It's like a picture is there, sounds are there, but they're floating just below the conscious level. Usually all the person is aware of is an unpleasant feeling. I should point out that a synesthesia is not always dysfunctional and is often associated with being resourceful. For example, Mozart used synesthesia in his creative strategies. When you're dealing with limiting beliefs, however, it's like your thoughts are globbed together in a single confusing representation where you can't see or hear clearly what's going on inside.

(*To Dee.*) You're afraid that somehow you'll get sucked into that "black hole" and you might never come out.

Dee. Yes.

Robert. And you want some sort of guarantee that you can go in and out of whatever the black hole represents?

Dee. Yes.

Robert. This one is saying no guarantees (Gestures to part) yet I wouldn't help you do it unless we could at least guarantee that you wouldn't be destroyed. How could you explore that and guarantee that you could go into that without being destroyed? What's the resource that you need? In other words . . .

Dee. I feel it's external to me . . . like there's something real out there that could destroy me.

Robert. Out where?

Dee. Out there in the distance (Gestures).

Robert. Is it inside of your memories, that distance?

Dee. No, it's in the distance out there (Gestures).

(*To Group.*) This is an interesting thing. Is it out there (Gestures away from Dee) or is it in here? (Points to her body.)

(*To Dee.*) Is it a part of you? We don't want you to be destroyed and we don't want to say something isn't real if it is real. You have some sort of sense of curiosity now . . .

Dee. Yes. I'm real curious.

Robert. How can you go about exploring something that's off in the distance without having it jeopardize your life? That's what you have eyes for, by the way. If I see something happening over there (Gestures away from Dee), by seeing it and knowing that it's there, I'm going to have more protection over my life than if I never go to it.

Dee. The problem is that it's dark. (Laughs)

Robert. It seems to me like there's a resource you need so that you don't have to go to it, but can look at it first. What if you have light? If you were to take some of the resources you have about visualizing to that situation, would it help?

Dee: Yes.

Robert: Do this. Put your eyes down here (Gestures to where Dee indicated that the black hole is located) so that you get a sense of what it is—and it's off there in the distance. It's not close enough to be dangerous. And keeping it the same distance, *look up* and see it out in the distance. Don't let it come any closer to jeopardize you.

Dee: Yes. It feels like it's a vortex.

Robert: What do you see? Don't feel it, see it.

Dee: It's hard to put light on it. I feel light all around it, but I don't feel light on *it*, and it feels like a vortex that could suck me in and destroy me.

Robert: It's a different kind of a "smoke screen." So you can't put any light on it. What is it? Maybe it's some other part of you.

Dee: OK. I see it now. It's a part that is very impulsive and crazy.

(*To Group*.) We've gotten down to an identity issue. She's saying "It's a part that could be me. I could fall into that and be impulsive and crazy." That's very real. I know people who have given in to those kinds of impulses. Those of you who work with others have probably seen people that act in that kind of a vortex. I mentioned earlier that some people will try to lock a part like that in their own insane asylum, or keep it in a cage so that they avoid it. By doing that, you're never going to be able to resolve the conflict and it will always be there, waiting to suck you into the vortex.

(*To Dee*.) What is that part of you out there trying to do for you? Does it want to suck you in and destroy you?

Dee: It's like the curiosity makes me want to go into it. It's like the curiosity is dangerous too.

Robert: Curiosity killed the cat (Dee has severe allergies to cats), but don't worry— they have nine lives. (Laughter)

In a sense there are two things going on here. This part itself is impulsive, it's not necessarily curious . . .

Dee: No. It's *very* dangerous. It's like it's all pure impulse. It doesn't think at all.

Robert: Is that what it *intends?* Ask that part if it intends to destroy you and suck you in and be completely impulsive.

Dee: No. It wants fun, excitement, and adventure.

Robert: So it wants fun, excitement and adventure. It doesn't want life threatening, vortex sucking destruction.

Dee: Right.

Robert: You let the cat out of the bag now, and you found out its teeth and claws are not as sharp as you thought. Did you ever have a cat when you were little?

Dee: No.

Robert: Did you ever have any animals?

Dee: No.

Robert: Ever since you can remember?

Dee: Yes.

Robert: So, this part wants fun and excitement and you have this other part with curiosity. It's the combination of being curious with the fun and excitement that would get you caught up into that. In other words, the vortex involves two things responding to each other. The vortex is not one part or the other. What resource would *you* need to be able to have fun and excitement, and all that part intends, but not get caught up in it and be destroyed? In other words, so you wouldn't lose your identity and get sucked into chaos?

Dee: My first thought was to analyze it, but when I analyze it, all the curiosity goes away.

Robert: So, when you analyze it, all the curiosity goes away and when you get curious, you don't have any analysis.

Dee: Right.

(*To Group:*) What we hear again are dissociated processes. How do we get analysis and curiosity together? Here are two resources that don't have any way of working together. Is it a strategy? How can you be curious and analytical simultaneously?

(*To Dee.*) Let's deal with the curious part. Where's your curious part?

Dee: I'm feeling curious now.

Robert: Oh! So you're curious. Where's the analytical part of you?

Dee: It's just kind of watching.

Robert: OK. Those two don't have much overlap with each other. Let's put one in each hand.

Dee: This one would be analysis (Gestures with the right hand). It's got a business suit on.

Robert: Probably appropriate. It has a business suit on. Let's go to this part. (Gestures to left hand.) What's the curious part of you like?

Dee: That's the artist.

Robert: So she's artistic.

Dee: Uh huh.

Robert: What does the other part of you look like out there? (Gestures) The "fun, exciting" part?

Dee: A lot of trouble (Laughs).

Robert: What does she look like out there?

Dee: I don't want to tell you. I need to censor that one (Laughing).

Robert: That's OK. We can tell by your physiology and your skin color change. Again we have dissociated experiences. What does the analytical one think of the other part as she looks over at the creative part?

Dee: She doesn't think about her very much. She's frivolous.

Robert: She thinks she's frivolous. Does this one (Gestures to left hand) intend to be frivolous?

Dee: Uh hum.

Robert: She wants to be frivolous? That's what her goal in life is?

Dee: Yes. She wants to be curious and to do paintings

and be creative and not make money.

Robert: And *not* make money, or is it that she doesn't care about money?

Dee: She doesn't care about money, and the result is that she doesn't make money.

Robert: Does she move away from money? That's the way you put it first.

Dee: No, she doesn't go away from it, she just gets involved in doing "things" that don't relate to making money. She is not altogether responsible. She doesn't pay bills and doesn't clean out the bathroom sink and . . .

Robert: But she's necessary too, though.

Dee: (Hesitation.)

Robert: Now have this one (Gestures to left hand) look at this one (Gestures to right hand).

Dee: She thinks the other one is boring.

Robert: Great! So you have a choice between being boring and frivolous (Laughter). This reminds me of a line from a Woody Allen book. He says "On the one hand we are headed toward utter destruction and doom, and on the other hand we face waste and lack of meaning. I hope to God we have the sense to make the right choice." (Laughter.)

(*To Group*:) You can begin to see how double binds occur. When she's doing the bathroom sink she's being responsible *but* boring. If she does the other, she's being creative and it gives some sort of meaning *but* she's being frivolous. It's back to being excitatory and inhibitory. We also have this other part (Gestures out) out there that we'll get back to.

We want to get to the point where we can figure out how to get each of these parts to work together.

(*To Dee*:) This one (Gestures to right hand) must also find resources in that one (Gestures to left hand).

Dee: She appreciates the creativity.

Robert: You see creativity can also be practical because

if you only stick to rote behaviors, you might do something that's impractical, just out of habit.

Dee: Uh hum.

Robert: Likewise, if you're going to be creative (Left hand), this one (Right hand) needs to implement that. This is the one that makes things happen in the real world.

Dee: She (Left hand) does have a real appreciation of that one (Right hand). She just thinks she's boring.

Robert: But she sees her value.

Dee: Yes, she sees her value.

Robert: What if you could get these two to not be separate anymore, but have a part of you that can be both creative and practical?

Dee: That's not possible.

Robert: What makes that impossible?

Dee: Because that's a compromise.

(*To Group:*) What we're hearing is we won't do that because then we have to compromise each other.

(*To Dee:*) I don't want you to compromise either one of them. In fact, right now, neither one of them is able to do their thing very well because the other one is always stopping them. How could you have a part of you that would have *full* resources of both, that's just as creative as this one (Left hand) but just as practical as this one (Right hand), where you don't have to give up anything? You only add resources. How could you create something so you have just as much of this (Right hand) as you have of that (Left hand)? What happens now is that they stop each other.

Do you know someone who is both creative and practical and is neither compromising, nor boring, nor frivolous?

Dee: I might know somebody. Can I make up somebody that I think might be that way?

Robert: Yes. What do they do? How do they balance and put these two things together so that neither of these is compromising and they have full access to the resources of all of them?

Dee: Hmm . . . I don't know that much about their life. Can I make it up?

Robert: Of course. You can do it so that this creative one (Left hand) can create some pieces and this one (Right hand) can test it out to see if it's practical. So the creative part comes up with the possibilities and the other part checks it out for you.

Dee: Oh! (Long pause) This creative one (Left hand) comes up with absolutely outrageous ideas that this one (Left hand) knows are absolutely not practical.

Robert: That's fine. So instead of rejecting the ideas, have this one (Right hand) refine them. The more impractical they are at first, the more they're going to allow for new possibilities. As you make them real, you might find that you come up with solutions that other people have gotten stuck on because they didn't start from such an outrageous point of view. Can you do that?

Dee: Uh huh. That's been going on. This one (Right hand) likes the ideas but doesn't want to implement them right now because of lack of money.

Robert: Go ahead and have her adjust those ideas so that either you can do them without money or so they'll *lead* you to money.

Dee: Oh! OK.

(*To Group:*) What was happening before we started negotiating between these parts was that the ideas were rejected out of hand. Now we have created a feedback frame between them. It all makes logical sense, but until it gets installed a person doesn't do it.

Dee: This one (Right hand) has to know where the money is, because it doesn't know.

Robert: That's where that one (Left hand) can help.

Dee: Uh, huh. (Her hands begin to move together with jerky ideomotor movements.)

(*To Group:*) You can see that she's not moving her hands consciously.

Dee. This is a very tentative relationship. (Laughter)

Robert: I can tell.

Dee. There's some trust, but not a whole lot.

Robert: What do they need to be able to trust one another?

Dee. Experience. They need to go ahead and experience each other's resources.

Robert: There's another piece that's still missing. Now we have all these ideas here, but where's the fun and excitement going to come in? Once you get a solid foundation and you start this integration going, then you don't have to be afraid. Think of it in terms of a chemistry metaphor. If I were to put two things together, I might get a chemical reaction. But if I add this, that and something else, then all of a sudden I get a solution that's completely different. There may be more to this than a chemistry metaphor, because you actually get brain chemical changes when you integrate together the neurological patterns associated with these parts.

Dee. (Her hands still moving together slowly.) This is weird (Laughing).

Robert: The weirder it is, the more you're on track.

Dee. OK. I'm not too sure about that! (Laughing)

Robert: That's the practical part (Right hand) speaking. You do need to be practical about that.

Dee. There's a part of me that wants to say, "Right on. Right on." This one (Right hand) is real unhappy with that one out there (Gestures out) and wants to shake a finger at it.

Robert: Oh. So this practical one (Right hand) is blaming that fun one out there.

Dee. She wants to admonish it and straighten it out.

Robert: Does this practical one (Right hand) understand that one's intention is not to do bad things and get admonished for it, but to make sure that you have fun and excitement?

Dee: Right. It understands it . . .

Robert: But it doesn't accept the way she's doing it.

Dee: Or that she *wants* to do it.

Robert: It doesn't trust *that's* what she wants.

Dee: Either that or that she'll do it the wrong way.

(*To Group:*) This is where some of the repression and conflict issues come in.

(*To Dee:*) Does that fun one (Gestures out) believe that it could have fun and excitement with both of these, if you brought that one in?

Dee: Uh huh. But this practical one doesn't believe that (Right hand). This one is real rigid and wants it done a specific way, which already doesn't work.

Robert: Does it know that?

Dee: Yes.

Robert: So, even though the practical one wants fun, it's still caught in that rigidity? Then it's acting in a way that it doesn't want to act. What resource does that part need in order to act differently?

Dee: It needs experience which it doesn't have.

Robert: How do you react in a situation where you don't have experience yet? This is a very important issue that centers around identity. You're going to be a different person. How are you going to be able to know what results are going to happen before you've tried it? The double bind of it is that you're thinking, "I'll trust it after I've experienced it, but I won't experience it until I trust it." I don't want to tell you, "Forget the trust part, just go ahead and do it." That's probably what this creative one (Left hand) would say, and that practical one (Right hand) would say, "No. Don't try anything."

Dee: Right. Exactly.

Robert: How can you do it? This creative one (Left hand) knows.

Dee: This creative one (Left hand) does know.

Dee: This adventurous one (Out there) will run films.

Robert: What would happen if this one were to run films of how to do it and how to have some of those experiences, and let that one (Right hand) evaluate it for practicality?

The creative one (Left hand) will start it, and that practical one (Right hand) will stop it and this adventurous one (Out there) will run a film about what's going to happen if it continues.

And this practical one (Right hand) will edit the film to make sure it's within the limits of practicality.

Dee: Yes. Then this creative one (Left hand) can give that one (Out there) more information.

Robert: It's a strategy.

Dee: Yes, and then this one (Out there) can run the film again and this practical one (Right hand) will approve or disapprove it.

Robert: If it disapproves, it doesn't have to reject . . . it can refine. It needs to say, "That's objectionable. Can you change part of it?"

Dee: That's right. Hum. That's interesting. This practical one's (Right hand) getting information, and can give information, and that one's (Out there) like the editor that can fit it all together.

Robert: Can you do that?

Dee: Yes.

Robert: Can you put them all together?

Dee: *They are* all together. Well. . . . that (Out there) one's still out there, but I guess that's OK.

Robert: We want to bring that one in too.

(*To Group*:) We want to make sure she has equal access to all of them. We want them integrated.

(*To Dee*:) How could you bring them in so that this part of you that used to be that tremendous black hole is a part of you? So that it's a part of an integrated you where you have access to all parts of you?

Dee: This part (Right hand) thinks that maybe we should just leave that part out there.

Robert: I believe that it does. But that's not going to work. What would you need to do now, to allow you to have a better quality experience? To be *more* practical than impractical?

Dee: OK. It's over here now (In the left hand).

Robert: So this part (Left hand) is both creative *and* fun. In essence, she's taking a smaller step. We're going to put this one (Out there) here (In left hand) first.

Dee: (Right hand is moving toward Left hand.)

Robert: This practical one (Right hand) is a little more anxious than this fun adventurous one (Left hand). Does this one (Left hand) still need something else? This one's afraid for it's own identity too.

Dee: I know what this one (Left hand) needs and I put it in.

Robert: Good. At this point I want to make sure that all objections have been met and they both feel comfortable coming together to form a new part for you. One that's both creative and fun and practical/analytical.

Dee: (Hands continue moving together with ideomotor movements.) It feels like they have no more objections and they're ready for each other.

Summary

(*To Group:*) As Dee continues integrating these aspects of herself, let me summarize the work we've done here. We started by clearing Dee's personal history via Re-imprinting. Sometimes when you do that, you're still left with parts in conflict. So, you begin by identifying the parts in conflict by watching for asymmetry in physiology and postures.

You then have the person make a full representation of each part, seeing, hearing and feeling them in each hand. Then have each part look at and consider the other. Often they'll have major objections to each other or they will mistrust each other.

Next, find the *positive intention* or outcome of each. Many times, they'll each think that the other part is negatively intended. It's critical to this process to get to the intentional level of each part. Typically, neither part will object to the intention of the other. Often you can continue working with both parts until they find a common intention that they could share—such as assuring that the person has a meaningful, worthwhile life.

Finally, have each part look at the other and realize what resources exist. You can have the person consider each "part" as a set of resources at this point. If the person has all these resources available, they'll certainly be a lot more effective. Getting congruent about what you want is one of the most important things you can do.

We also want the person to realize that if the parts combine their resources, they'll be much more powerful as a single integrated whole that can accomplish their higher purposes and their common goal.

The intention allows them to begin to share resources so that we get the best of both working towards their common shared goal. So at this point we see the parts coming together to become a unified part to make the person whole. That kind of feeling—being a "whole person" is something that's not easy to describe because it's "just you."

Questions

Man: You mentioned that we should test when the integration is complete. How do you test?

Robert: As Dee's hands came together, I asked her a series of questions about her ability to make money and do practical things in a fun, creative way. Dee's responses were congruently positive and she gestured with both hands in harmonious movements.

To find out if the integration is whole and complete, I begin to engage the person in appropriate activities. If it was smoking that they were dealing with, I would have them go back and think about smoking and notice what happens.

Then I watch for an integrated physiology. If they are verbalizing that the picture of the new part is integrated, but I notice that their body is not, I go with the physiology and know that it's not complete yet.

Of course, a behavioral test is always the best. If you can actually put the person into the situation that used to create problems and you get a new and congruent response, you know that something has shifted and integration has taken place.

Woman: Dee seemed to be confused at times during this process. What about that?

Robert: There is a difference between "good" confusion and "bad" confusion. Sometimes when people get confused, it's because they've just integrated. Sometimes it's because they're disintegrated. In both cases, their thoughts and feelings will seem different, not familiar, and they won't understand what's going on.

Some confusion is good. When you've just integrated conflicting parts, the world literally isn't the same. Things seem very different. Conversely, there are other times when it seems like you're torn between internal parts, and you don't know whether to go this way or that way. That's the kind of confusion that will keep you stuck.

Woman: Why do you put the parts in the hands?

Robert: The reason I have someone put their "part" in a hand and talk to it is because I want to take something that is just a feeling and add visual and auditory representations to it. I want them to access more of the brain than when it is just a feeling. I also do that as a natural outgrowth of asymmetrical gesturing.

Also, when you have the person see, hear and feel the part in their hand, you are having them consider the part and its intention from a "meta position." Instead of being caught up in it, they are outside it, considering it in a different way and gaining a new perspective.

Man: How do you know when to go for an imprint versus doing a conflict resolution?

Robert: If the behavior is oriented heavily towards asymmetry and it shifts from right to left, I'll go with congruency issues. If someone is more symmetrical, but has lots of intense physiology associated with the behavior, that lets me know it's probably an imprint.

Woman: You've talked about asymmetry. Are there other physiological cues to watch for or use?

Robert: Sometimes when the person is in a conflicted state, he will have trouble moving his eyes from one eye accessing position to another. You'll often find a different physiology associated with each eye movement. When he describes one belief he might be looking up and left. When he describes the conflicting belief, he might shift his eyes down and right. If he has physiology that is very different for each aspect of his identity, you can bet that he'll have mental processes that will be very different as well.

When I am working with people, I frequently ask the question, "What stops you from achieving your desired outcome?" I then look for an immediate unconscious physiological response that comes before they have a chance to consciously think about it. (This is called the half-second rule.) I'm not as interested in the verbal answer as I am the non-verbal cues that occur in the first half-second that let me know precisely how the person is getting stuck.

Sometimes you'll find a discontinuity in eye movements when a person moves her eyes from one position to another. When she moves her eyes from V^r (up and left) to K (down and right) and you find a hesitation or a deviation in direction, it's a communication that something isn't integrated appropriately.

When you find a discontinuity in eye movements, the

first step is to start integrating the two physiologies together. Your goal is to help her move easily from one eye quadrant to the other. You can do that by having her access and totally get into one state and while holding that state, have her move her eyes to the conflicting quadrant. Your outcome is to assist her in literally creating an access between the two quadrants. This installs a new pathway for accessing her resources and gives her more choices about her beliefs and behaviors.

So, one way that you can move towards integration is to create a smooth movement between the two polarities, and eye accessing cues give you an avenue for doing that.

You can also move toward integration using voice tones. Have her start with one voice tone and then slowly change the tone or tempo until it goes to the other one. The whole idea is to create connections between the two conflicting parts.

The best time to install this smooth pathway (either visually or auditorially), is when she is to the point of saying, "I don't know what to do." That signifies an impasse, and connecting the two together will often make an incredible difference.

The Conflict Integration Model Summary

1. Identify the conflicting beliefs and calibrate to the physiologies of each of the parts in conflict. (Pay particular attention to asymmetries.)

2. Represent the beliefs in all sensory systems, putting the different beliefs in different hands. See the you with 'X' belief in your right hand. See the you with 'Y' belief in the other hand. Find out what images, voices, sounds and feelings are associated with each part.

3. Ask each part to look at the other and describe what it sees. At this stage, the different parts will often dislike and

mistrust each other. You should see the person display different physiologies as he/she switches back and forth between hands.

4. Find out the positive intention and purpose of each part. Make sure that each part recognizes and accepts the positive intent of the other. Point out that their conflict is directly interfering with the achievement of their own positive intentions. If necessary, go to the higher level intention of each.

5. Identify the common goal that they both share.

6. Have each part look at the other and describe the resources that the other has that would be helpful to that part. Secure a congruent agreement from the parts to combine their resources so they can more fully achieve their positive intentions.

7. If the image of either of the parts has been metaphorical, see the part as your own likeness at this point.

8. Suggest that the parts move together at the same time that a new identity is being created. Get a full representation in all sensory systems that fully integrates the resources of both parts. Calibrate to an integration/symmetry of the two physiologies that accompanied the separate parts.

9. After the hands have moved together and integration is complete, test in future contexts to make sure that there are no further ecology issues.

ENDNOTES

1. See John Grinder & Richard Bandler, *The Structure of Magic II* (Palo Alto, CA: Science and Behavior Books, 1975), pp. 62-96.

6

Criteria

Criteria and values are a special category of beliefs. They are the beliefs you hold about *why* something is important or worthwhile. They are very powerful and individualized.

Write down, as if you were answering aloud, your response to the following question: "What do you want in a job?" The words that come to mind will represent your criteria for a job. If these criteria aren't largely satisfied by your position, you'll be unhappy in your work. You can demonstrate the power of these criteria for yourself by asking a friend the same question and jotting down her list of criteria. Pretend you are assigning her a job task first using *your* criteria words, then assign her the same task using her specific words. Unless they are the same precise words, you'll see a big difference in her physiology. If you want to turn someone on about something, use *their* criteria, not your own.

Sometimes people have problems in the way that they think about and internally represent their criteria. These problems can be related to : (1) Hierarchy; (2) Degree; (3) Chunk size; (4) Identity and (5) Conflicts.

Hierarchy of Criteria

It's important to remember that each of us arrange our criteria hierarchically. For example, say that having fun and earning a living are both important to you. Earning a living might be more important than having fun, so you don't cut work to go skiing.

You can have problems when your own internal hierarchy is not ordered in a way to best serve you. For example, if your enjoyment of sweets is more important than your health, you may gain a lot of weight and become unhealthy.

Degree

There is the issue of degree in dealing with criteria. For example, if earning a living is typically more important for you than having fun, but you are faced with choosing an activity that is *really* fun or one that will earn you only a little income, you might choose the fun activity.

People can have problems when they are confused about this issue of degree in their thinking. For example, some people will always preclude having fun in order to earn money. They may come to see you because they are dissatisfied with their lives.

Chunk Size

Sometimes people have vague definitions for their criteria. For example, a person might say, "It's important to be healthy." You ask, "What do you mean by being healthy?" In order to answer you, they'll need to come up with another list of criteria, such as having high energy, weighing within a certain range, feeling a certain way, etc. When people haven't thought through how they'll know if a certain criteria is being met, or what the sub-criteria or criteria equivalence are, they may feel confused about how to achieve what they want or they may be overwhelmed by the idea of achieving it. If you break a criteria down into its component parts, you'll know what it is and what it takes to satisfy it.

Identity and Criteria

If, when planning to buy a car, you decide that a sports car would represent the "new you" and a station wagon would represent your responsibility to your family, then you're not just dealing with criteria, you're dealing with your identity.

Let me use smoking as another example. Some people quit smoking because it bothers other people. They quit because the criteria of having others appreciate them carries more weight than the pleasure they get from smoking. They're using their criteria to alter a behavior. There are others, however, that complicate the issue by saying, "If I can quit smoking, I can do anything. I can really be the person I've always wanted to be." If you're working with the first person you're helping them to change a habit, a behavior. If you're working with the second, you'll be dealing with *who* the person *is* and *who* they'll become, and the issue will be much more complex.

Conflicts of Criteria

Conflicts inside us are often conflicts of criteria. For example, you want to do activities that are fun, but you have to earn a living. If you have defined these activities in an "either/or" way to yourself, having one will preclude having the other. You will feel cheated, regardless of which activity you choose.

With that brief background on criteria and values, I'd like to explore an issue where a person wants to make a particular change, but stops himself; starts to change but runs out of steam; or gets into some kind of conflict when he tries to implement the change. A common example of the kind of issue I'm talking about is when you have decided to exercise, but when the time comes, that plan disappears and something else pops up that you would rather do. When this occurs there is almost always a conflict of criteria. Who has an issue like that?

Conflicting Criteria Demonstration

Robert: Mary— why don't you come up here.

Mary: Whenever I start a diet, I follow it for a few days and then the whole plan begins to fall apart.

(*To Group:*) So, Mary has a problem where she decides to get started on something that she wants to do, but then doesn't follow through.

Her real outcome is not just to lose weight, but to establish new eating patterns. Dieting often won't work for a long term success because it doesn't necessarily result in better behavior patterns. What is the word "DIET" anyway? It's die with a "t" on the end. I don't think diets are the most effective way of losing weight. When you lose weight, you lose muscle tissue first and *then* fat. When you begin to re-gain weight, fat comes back before you develop muscle. Your weight will go up and down while your body tries to reach homeostasis; a balance of muscle and fat. There are lots of people who have lost thousands of pounds in their lives dieting, only to put it all back on again. I call this the "rhythm method of girth control."

What you need to do to gain and maintain a healthy weight for yourself is to organize your eating strategy and your criteria so they really work in the way you want them to.

(*To Mary:*) You said that you diet and lose weight to a certain point and then something happens. What is it that happens? Do you start losing willpower, or do you start getting frustrated? What specifically happens?

Mary: I maintain the new weight for a while and then I stop trying and gain it back. One of the things that occurred to me as you were talking a moment ago is that about a year ago, I stopped a diet after carefully controlling what I ate for 18 months. I decided to just let my body reach its natural weight, and since then I've gained weight like crazy.

Robert: You're talking about just letting the body do what it wants to do. But what we are really talking about is harmonizing your mind and your body.

Your goal is not just to lose weight but to be a thinner person, right? (Mary affirms by nodding) What would being a thin person do for you?

Mary: I want to move easily and look nice in my clothes. But even more importantly, I want to feel nice in my clothes. I also want to be congruent professionally. As a therapist, I want to have my act together in relation to my weight and appearance.

(*To Group*:) In all my work, I am gathering information non-verbally as we are forming her outcome. Eye accessing cues represent one way in which she is offering us information. When she talks about moving easily she moves her eyes down, not exactly a straight kinesthetic access, but down in that direction.

(*To Mary*:) What are you aware of when you think about moving easily?

Mary: I'm aware of the way it feels to move, mainly. But I have a sense that there is something up there as well (Points up and to her right).

Robert: So you have a feeling and some kind of vague visual construct. You want to look nice. How do you think of that?

Mary: (Eyes move up and right) I don't visualize well, but I'm aware of a flash of color and some movement. My experience is that when I think about this it's all pretty vague in terms of any images.

(*To Group:*) There is a general principle that is important to mention at this point. When you interview people that are very good at something, it is common for them to have a clear, highly detailed representation of whatever it is they do well. They represent their successes vividly. When you ask them about their failures, they often have vague representations of those and there is hardly any physiological response.

On the contrary, if you ask someone who is having trouble doing something about their successes, they will describe them as very vague internal representations, and will display very little physiology. Ask about the times they've failed and you'll get all kinds of detailed representations.

I've been talking recently with a company called Sybervision. Among other things, they create videos for sports performance. They are using a number of NLP discoveries and methods. One of the methods they use is to show images, like that of a correct golf swing, over and over, so that the trainee has a reference image to use as a model. The more your brain senses something, and the more levels of detail that you have, the more you're going to be able to do it, whether it's success or failure.

(*To Mary:*) What's this image that you have? Associated or dissociated? Like something that you have seen before or more like a construct?

Mary: Like a construct.

Robert: How about feeling nice in your clothes?

Mary: (Eyes down right) I have more experience with this. I can feel it.

Robert: OK. When you think about the notion of professional congruence, what happens on the inside?

Mary: Again, I'm not sure what I'm doing on the inside. I have a very good sense about myself as a therapist, and I have lots of pictures and images about times when I have done effective work. Somehow these images don't match with my having extra weight.

Robert: You are talking about some kind of comparison. What is being compared? Are you comparing pictures to each other, or pictures to a feeling in your body?

Mary: The pictures don't match my feelings about myself.

Robert: Mary, think of a time when you had the opportunity to stay with new eating habits or go back to your old ones, and the old ones won out. What happened there?

Mary: I can sometimes stay just a little above what I have set as my goal weight. When I get close, it's almost like there is a barrier. The closer I approach it, the more I pull away from it.

Robert: What sort of thing happens specifically when you pull away? How does "pulling away" manifest itself? Give me a context.

Mary: A sense that people would look more at me than sense me.

Robert: What does that criteria mean to you? Does that mean that you don't want to be judged? That they would know the real you . . . ?

Mary: It's like they would see me superficially and then lose track of what I feel I am.

Robert: So lose track of what you feel you are. Is there more?

Mary: I really like variety in food choices and intense foods. If I don't pull away, I fear that I would lose that in my life.

Robert: Lose variety. Lose track of who you are. Here are a couple of "away from" Meta-sorts. These are matched negatives. She is trying to avoid a match to a negative. Hitting her desired weight would mean that people would lose sense of who she is and that she would be a person who did not have certain kinds of variety in her life.

Robert: When you worry about people responding to you

superficially and not to who you really are, how do you become concerned?

Mary: I feel like I somehow change position in relation to myself. That I am somehow dissociating in the image of myself as well. I also hear a phrase in my mind, one that I thought I had dealt with before. One time when I got down to a weight that was more like my natural weight, my husband said that no matter how much weight I lost, I would still be pear shaped.

Robert: Ah ha! So there's an A (auditory remembered) with a pretty big K (kinesthetic) there. What else? You said you somehow "changed position."

You are still in this negative feeling aren't you? So we have this set of representations and all of a sudden there is this negative K feeling which is not like the other representations. It's more like a K squared, a "mega-feeling."

So you heard that voice and got that bad feeling. Was that all that you heard, or was there another voice or statement? Did that voice bring up other memories or thoughts?

Mary: (Looks up and to the right) Um . . . the pear shape that I see in my mind's eye is the shape that I see on my mother.

Robert: Is it a remembered image?

(*To Group:*) She's got a pear shape there. *Now* she is saying that she sees that.

(*To Mary:*) Do you literally see that? Is it a clear image? I saw you tracing that shape in the air.

Mary: It is certainly clearer than an image I could make about my ideal self.

Robert: When you see that shape, do you also see an image of your mother? How do you relate it to your mother?

Mary: I can see pictures of her fading in and out, when she was not dressed. I see a number of times.

Robert: How many pictures would you say that you have?

Mary: Two or three of them.

Robert: So three V^r (visual remembered) pictures.

(*To Group:*) We can look at the way she is representing these experiences and begin to notice that the representations are unequal. In her desired state images, she had only a flash of color and a sense of movement. Here, she has a much richer representation. It is literally represented differently. What we need to do is to balance them out and equalize the equation.

(*To Mary:*) Let's take the variety issue. How do you think about losing variety?

Mary: That is tied up with the diet notion. Diets restrict your choices.

Robert: What's there?

Mary: It's like an either/or situation. It's not like I can have variety and smaller amounts. It's like either I can have variety, or I can't have enough.

Robert: All I need to know at this point is when you are worried about losing variety, what is that like? What happens inside of you?

Mary: I don't see any pictures, but if I look up there (Looks up and to her right) I don't have nearly the struggle about losing variety.

Robert: So somehow variety is associated with this internal auditory thing. Put your eyes down there (Gestures to her left). How will you lose variety?

Mary: I don't have any words, just a lot of thundering in my ears.

Robert: OK, a thundering noise.

(*To Group:*) As we watch her accessing, we know that her representation is clearly auditory dialogue. We are, however, just concerned about the structure for the time being. We have two sides to the equation, here.

Here is the last step before we start to put all of this together. We want to find an internal representation that is greater than the voice of her husband saying she is pear shaped and the remembered picture of her mother's body looking pear shaped.

(*To Mary:*) Has there ever been a time when you have done something that resulted in a loss of variety and that you would do again, even though your choices would be restricted?

Mary: Learning! Learning, learning, learning, learning.

Robert: Learning! And we have five of them. How do you think about learning?

Mary: I can lose track of myself, and get lost in the task, or I can do a task that someone else assigns me to do. Like when you assigned us a task to do in the training seminar yesterday. I could think of other ways to do the assignment. It was easy to restrict myself to the approach that you suggested because I wanted to learn your approach. (Mary's voice speeds up, and is slightly higher, indicating visual accessing.)

(*To Group:*) As she talks, I can see her accessing more places.

(*To Mary:*) When you are describing that, what is going on inside? You have words, clearly, and also those words have a certain voice tone and tempo.

Mary: I feel a lot more movement. I feel a lot looser.

Robert: How do you know to feel looser? Does that feeling come from words, or pictures?

Mary: It's a very sparkly sense. I feel like I can really move.

Robert: It's a sparkly sense. You said learning, learning, learning, learning, learning, and then you made a statement to yourself. What do you say to yourself?

Mary: I can't actually hear all of the words that I say to myself, but there is a lot of rhythm to them. There is also a sense of a lot of verbal flexibility.

(*To Group:*) OK. The idea of learning overrides not having variety. It has an auditory component, a kinesthetic component and a visual component; all with identified submodalities. We have enough information now to select a specific process to use to assist Mary in making the change that she wants. There are at least three different methods that we can use that would utilize this criteria alone.

One of them is called leveraging. Leveraging in this case means to take the higher criteria identified in the situation where she will restrict choice (learning) and apply it to eating.

We know that the criteria of learning would override the criteria for variety, yet she is not applying it to gain the kind of weight she wants to gain.

Mary: I like that, "Gaining the weight I want" sounds so much better than "losing weight" does.

Robert: And it can sound louder too. How can you make being the weight you want, looking nice, feeling nice, and being in balance, a learning task? Isn't that something that you need to *learn* to do as well?

Mary: I have been studying body work, and I'm aware of doing lots of learning in a body sense.

Robert: How can you learn to be the weight you want, without having to lose some sense of self or variety?

Mary: I believe that it is possible, but I don't have evidence that I can do it.

Robert: Do you have evidence that you can learn to do it?

Mary: Hm . . . I have evidence that I have learned lots of things.

Robert: Whether you have evidence or not is not relevant to learning. When you set out to learn something, you don't know what is going to happen. You do know that there are other ways to do something. It is easy for you to just go for it.

Mary: I still have a feeling here (Points to her midline).

Robert: You have this feeling here (Points to the midline) that you won't be able to do it. Notice that this feeling does not fit anywhere in the representation of learning. Where does that come from? That's different than you'll lose yourself or you won't have variety. It sounds like a belief that you won't be able to do it. Where does that feeling come from?

Mary: Here. (Points to midline in chest area.) It's like I breathe it and feel it here. (Her eyes tear and color increases.)

Robert: (Helps her break state by touching her arm gently) OK. By the way, I can see from your physiology that this is probably the most congruent feeling that you are having. There is another issue here too. You talk about being pear shaped. (She again shows the physiology of the midline feeling.) In *NLP Volume I* we described a person who has a pear shape as having a particular kind of strategy.[1] Pear shaped people generally use a visual-kinesthetic strategy; visual on the top and kinesthetic on the bottom, where kinesthetic is indeed the bottom line.

(*To Mary:*) When you change your weight, you are changing your strategy. You are becoming a different person. The way that you think is different. Visual accessing begins to take more precedence than the kinesthetics in certain respects, but that doesn't mean that you lose your kinesthetic sense. Pear shaped people tend to lead visually, but feelings are the bottom line. So when you talk about gaining the weight that you want, you are talking about being a different person. That is allowing the visual to be more a part of who you are as well.

Mary: My mind is going to learn, learn, learn, learn, learn.

Robert: Right. When I lost weight, it had to be all right with me to be a different person. There were a number of issues that I had to deal with in regard to learning to be a new person. The feeling that you now are having is certainly a pure kinesthetic. That's an important piece of information to have. Is it an old feeling? . . .

Mary: . . . It's like, because that is the way my mother's body looks, it's the way that mine has to look as well. I feel really disheartened by that (Eyes tear).

Robert: (Anchors the feeling) Let's go back with that and stay with that feeling for a while. When did you first get that feeling? Where does that feeling come from, and what beliefs are associated with it?

Mary: In my family there were a lot of genealogical interests, and a lot of comparing of the children to our parents.

Robert: Do you get that feeling when you think about those discussions? There is a lot of feeling there.

Mary: No.

Robert: Go back to where you got that feeling.

Mary: . . . There was some time right around my early adolescence when my mom forced me to have an enema. I don't even know if there was a medical reason or not. I remember screaming and telling her not to do it, and she did it anyway. (Begins to cry.)

Robert: That's all right. What belief did you build from that experience?

Mary: That she would win and I would lose.

Robert: Now, we can come all the way back to 1986. (Breaks state as he pats her gently on the arm).

(*To Group:*) Notice that there has been a theme of "losing self" throughout Mary's descriptions. When you have a mega-feeling, an extremely intense K, it is usually a result of an imprint. My question when I get such a big K from a person is, "Why is this particular criteria so important to the person?"

For example, why does someone think that personal responsibility to their family is so much more important than taking care of themselves? The reason why someone tries to hold on to something so hard is because of imprint type experiences. This is the case nine times out of ten. When an incident like the enema situation occurs it is usually when the person is forming an opinion about identity.

Do you think that your mother had an idea about your response? There are a lot of times when the parent imposes their will on the child and there is no resulting imprint. There are times, however, that determine something about *who* you are as a person. That's what makes this incident an imprint. This may have become an imprint issue because you didn't know what was going on and it became a case of willpower.

(*To Mary:*) I'd like you to see that "younger you" in puberty with your mother with the altercation going on. Are you friend or are you enema? Can you change this animosity? (Laughter) . . . The shit is going to fly now. All right, as you look at that now, are there any other generalizations that you formed?

Mary: That she doesn't understand me; she doesn't believe me.

Robert: She doesn't understand me. She doesn't believe me.

That is another set of complex equivalencies. Was your mother's intention to make you lose, to not believe you and to lead you into the difficulties that you have today?

Mary: No.

Robert: As you look back to that time now, what do you think that her intention was?

Mary: I think that she was doing what she thought she had to do. I think it became a control issue for her when I resisted.

Robert: The reason that I am going into this is because control issues are common problems when people have difficulty maintaining the weight they want. People develop a kind of internal saboteur whose function is to maintain control. This part will find some way of resisting. So you get the enema and you are going to hold it just as long as you can just to show your mother.

(*To Group:*) I remember going through my puberty and having similar kinds of issues. My dad would come into my room in the morning and say, "Get up, it's time for school." I didn't want to get up because *he* told me to. I was going to get up because *I* wanted to. So I'd wait for five minutes, and then I could get up because I wanted to. Four and one half minutes later, he would call me again to get up. Then I had to wait another five minutes. It had started to become a control issue. I re-imprinted myself on that one, by the way.

(*To Mary:*) So your mother's intent was not a win-lose battle. What was it that your mother needed then, so that this experience could have been more positive for both of you? So that the incident never would have gotten to the point of a win-lose situation?

Mary: She needed to teach me how to do it myself. She would have needed to explain to me why it had to be done as well. At that age I could have done it myself.

Robert: I hear a learning issue involved here, too. So she needs to know that you like to learn and she needs to teach you. She also needs to recognize that you are at that age where you can start to take care of yourself. Mary, I know there are times for you when you are working with your clients that you recognize when they need to do things for themselves. Times when they need to be taught how to do something, and not just have something done for them. Think of a time when you were really able to have that sense, maybe even as a child.

Mary: Yes, I have a time like that . . . (Robert anchors her state as she accesses a time.)

Robert: Now, let's hold that anchor and look back at your mother as you give her some of that resource. How would she have dealt with that situation differently? . . .

Mary: Her whole voice tone changes. She would have taken me to another room and explained what was going on. She is calm and patient.

Robert: What happens to the younger you? How does she respond?

Mary: With a sense of relief and curiosity.

Robert: OK, good. I'd like you to replay the whole thing again. Now that your mother is acting in a patient, under- standing way, how do you respond? I don't think that your intention as a child was to create a response that would bother you for the rest of your life. What resource did that younger you need at that time so that the situation would not have become this unpleasant imprint experience?

Mary: I needed to make it clear that I needed more information.

Robert: You needed to make it clear that you wanted knowledge from your mom. Having an enema wasn't the problem. Your mother needed to know that it is not a power issue, but an information issue.

Have you ever needed to do that with somebody? Where you were able to validate their intention as well as your own intention and get on to what was important?

Mary: The answer is yes, but I can't think of a particular time.

Robert: Of course, it *is important* to get a specific example. So it would have been a time when something was confusing to you and you needed to make that clear without getting into a useless power struggle . . . a time when you recognized that could have happened . . . a time when you said to the other person, "I understand that your intention is thus and so, but I need to have something cleared up first." It could have been with a doctor, a teacher, or anybody else.

Mary: I remember when I was in the doctor's office and there was some kind of procedure that they wanted to do. I asked them to explain it all so I would understand the implications before having it done. I wanted to know what would happen and what all of the alternatives were. I wasn't resisting them; I just wanted the information.

(*To Group*:) Mary said earlier, in relation to trying to diet that she started to "shift position." When she shifts position, losing weight becomes something she doesn't want to do.

What does an imprint do? You start shifting position with the other person from your past. Then losing weight becomes not something that you want to do, but something that is being done to you. It's something to resist, to preserve your integrity. The purpose of doing the re-imprinting is that if you shift perspectives either way, you will have the appropriate resources.

(*To Mary:*) What was it like when you queried the doctor? How did you know that you could do that? What kind of belief do you have now that allowed you to do that?

Mary: I could. I believe that I am confident enough and articulate enough to ask the necessary questions to satisfy my needs in that situation. Also, I believe I am sufficiently aware of my needs to express them.

Robert: OK. Let's give that set of resources to that younger you, back in the situation with your mother. (Holds the resource anchor) What does that younger you do differently?

Mary: Well, for one thing she doesn't get hysterical and scream and cry. She talks instead.

Robert: My guess is that we have a completely different impact on your mother as well. (Pronoun we)

Mary: I could also feel my whole body loosen up. That means that the whole impact of the enema would have been different, because my body would not have been so tight.

Robert: What I want you to do now is to go back to the scene with your mother and step into her and see through her eyes. Give her the resource of knowing when someone needs to be taught. (He touches the previously established resource anchor.) Go through what you saw and hear what you were saying.

Mary: This is different.

Robert: (Continues to touch the anchor) Now, get this from the perspective of the little girl. Step into her. . . . Mary, you said that the belief you had formed as a result of that experience was that your mom didn't understand or believe you. What belief do you have now?

Mary: Well, one of the things that I told her when I was reliving the experience was that I was scared. I told my mom that she didn't know much about being scared and suggested we talk about that. It was like both of us gained something new and useful.

Robert: So, how would you put that into a statement of belief?

Mary: If we both learn what is important to each of us, then everybody wins. And that is how it feels now.

Robert: One more thing for you to do. Put your eyes down here now. (Gestures down and to her right, indicating that he wants her to access kinesthetically) I want you to repeat all these beliefs that you feel while looking there. That you are intelligent . . . that you can both win . . . that you are capable enough and important enough . . . (Holds all the resource anchors).

Mary: It is a belief that I already have in lots of other situations. It's not hard to do this.

Robert: OK. Let's come all the way back to the present time and place. You also mentioned a time when your husband said that no matter how much weight you lose, you are still going to be pear shaped. What happens when you hear that now? I don't know anything about his intention. What do you think it was?

Mary: He would be harder to teach. (Laughter)

Robert: Virginia Satir has said that people are slow but they are educable. When you mentioned that your husband said that, there were clearly some feelings there. What were those feelings?

Mary: It was like "Here I am, reaching some success and he says that." I lose again. I felt like a failure.

Robert: A double bind. "Even when I win, I fail to the people who are important to me." What do you suppose his intention was? I heard a man say to his wife who was losing weight, "I'm going to love you no matter what you look like, but I'm glad that you are losing weight." Which one is the true statement? It is a paradox, right? He is going to love her no matter what she looks like, and yet he is pleased that she is making an effort to look nice and to take care of herself.

Robert: What do you think your husband's intentions were in saying that no matter how much weight you lost you'd still be pear shaped?

Mary: His intentions were to be controlling of me. That's why he is my ex-husband.

Robert: He was frightened about your losing weight and looking good?

Mary: Yes.

Robert: He was going "Oh, Oh, she is going to be too independent."

(*To Group*:) I often get similar issues from others when working on weight problems.

One woman said, "If I exercise, eat right, and really feel good about myself, I'll lose the people that I care about." When we went back to the imprint situation from a previous marriage, we found that the marriage was based on a dependency relationship. When the woman started to grow in the sense of her own personal evolution, her husband got worried, and eventually the marriage got into trouble. The better she felt about herself, the more alienated her husband became. She began to orient away from the relationship by finding new friends and becoming involved in new activities. Eventually the marriage broke up. She was not aware of what the issues were until after the marriage dissolved. She did have a belief that if she did things for herself that she'd ruin her most important relationships.

Mary: I think that when I chose him as my husband, I felt that I needed to be controlled on some level. Those issues have been resolved now.

Robert: We still need to deal with that auditory remembered statement about your weight and being pear shaped. You have this memory about your husband saying this and you get this big negative feeling. The belief has less to do with how you look than what was going on in that relationship.

(He shifts the tone of voice that he has been using to the soft tone he used with the last resource anchor he used, and touches the spot he anchored earlier when he re-imprinted the enema memory.) We could re-imprint this, but instead of that, listen to the voice again and have a different experience. (Mary hears the statement in her mind again while maintaining the resourceful physiology.)

(*To Group.*) I want to backtrack what we have done so far. We began by "leveraging" Mary's criteria, but we ran into an imprint—a big feeling that needed to be re-imprinted before we could go on. Leveraging criteria is one way to identify imprints and find out where to tap. We have completed the re-imprinting, and now I want to ask Mary some additional questions related to the criteria she offered us earlier.

(*To Mary:*) Mary, do you believe that you can move easily, look nice, feel nice, be balanced with the way that you feel inside and the way you look outside, in that natural way? In a way that you don't lose track of yourself? In fact, in a way that you can keep track of your real self . . . having variety, eating appropriately and learning how to do this in a good way for you?

Mary: (Very congruently) Yes!

Robert: What we want to do now is take the goal that you have of being balanced, looking nice, feeling nice, moving easily, keeping track of yourself and having variety, and make it match the structure of your criteria for learning. We are going to do this literally on the level of submodalities and physiology. You really know when you learn because there is a certain sparkle to your representation. There is a quality of movement to it. There is a set of words with a particular quality. What I want you to do is to think of what you would like to be like. Learning takes a certain amount of time. Rather than go on a diet, can you learn to be the person that you want to be?

When I lost my 30 pounds, I didn't want to go on a diet. I wanted to be the person that I am now. I thought, "I'm not on a diet now, so why should I go on a diet?" My losing weight had to do with me becoming a different person in many ways.

I remember a woman who said, "I quit smoking a lot of times, but I wasn't successful at quitting until I became a non-smoker." In other words, until "it became me" to be a non-smoker.

Let's finish backtracking what we have accomplished so far. Mary, you want your body to be congruent with your professional identity. Before the re-imprinting, however, your pictures of yourself as an effective therapist didn't match your feeling about yourself. Furthermore, you seemed to be concerned that people would *look* more at you than "sense" who you really were. Your husband's comment that you would always be pear shaped no matter how much weight you lost presents an interesting paradox in this respect. On one hand, he failed to sense the "real you" that you experience professionally. On the other hand, perhaps he touched upon a "real you" that you felt associated with; even imposed on you by your mother, as a result of an adolescent imprint. I thought it was interesting that you said the image of her body was more clear than any image you could make about your "ideal" self. That seemed to indicate that your image of the professional you was actually more of an idealization than the "real" you. This creates a "V-K split" that manifests itself in the "pear shape" visual on the top and kinesthetic on the bottom. The re-imprinting we have done has brought these two more into balance by adding in resources from the auditory system in the form of your ability to articulate your need for information and ask questions.

Now that we have cleared out the limiting beliefs from your personal history through the re-imprinting process you are now free to "learn, learn, learn, learn, learn" about being a thinner more symmetrical person. Several times when you mentioned your learning resources you used that word "learn" five times. The fact that there are five seems important to me and I would like to incorporate it in where you go from here.

First of all, we each have five senses, and it seems to me that, in regard to becoming a thinner person, there is something to learn in each of those senses. Secondly, there are five levels on which to learn; that of environment, behavior, capability, belief, and identity. Your five senses form a horizontal dimension for learning, and the five levels form a vertical dimension. So, in order to "learn, learn, learn, learn, learn," you would want to find out what you would see, hear, feel, smell and taste in your environment, your behavior, your capabilities, your beliefs and your identity that would help you become lighter and more balanced. That ought to give you quite a *variety*.

Mary: Hmmm. Sounds like an interesting approach.

Robert: That's right. And you can feel free to restrict yourself just to the parts of the approach that will give you more variety in gaining what you want to gain, as you did with the assignment you mentioned from the other day.

Now, I'd like you to take a moment and put yourself into a comfortable position. And go deeply inside of yourself to a place where you can learn fully and completely (Pause). That's right. Fully sense what it is like to have a congruent and coordinated identity. Feel and hear the resourceful, professional qualities that embody the way you know you really are inside. Visualize how you look as you manifest those qualities. See the shape and quality of movement that you have, not as an ideal image but a natural, normal image that fits with who you already are. Take a deep breath and breathe that image inside of you, so that it becomes a part of you. Notice the smell and taste it leaves in your mouth. Let that smell and taste be a guide for you to know what to eat in the future.

Now, review the beliefs that you will need, and have, that support this congruent, balanced person. When all parts and aspects of you learn what is important to them, all of you wins. *That* you can sense when you need to learn something and articulate the questions you need to ask to get the appropriate information. *That* you can have the variety you love in many, many ways (in addition to eating). Allow your mind to drift over your life experiences and find examples of times that you've done this before. Feel the feelings that let you know you need information. Feel the curiosity that motivates you to pursue the information you need. Hear the tone of voice that is confident and knows that you are aware of your true needs and can satisfy them. See the situations in your mind, all of those situations where you've been able to successfully meet your needs, over and over again . . . each situation, having its own unique flavor. Feast your eyes on all those situations where you've been able to follow the scent of your own needs, and fill yourself with the appropriate amount of information.

Review the capabilities that you have that support this identity and those beliefs. The ability to learn through all of your senses. To eat up the world around you with your eyes and ears and be filled with a sense of curiosity and excitement. To find all the choices available to you to expand and enrich your map of the world, so there is more space for you to move easily and comfortably. To model others who have been able to successfully balance their personal and professional identity in an ecological and harmonious way. The ability to lose yourself in what you are doing and just follow your nose. That's right . . . your unconscious knows. The ability to talk and ask questions in order to satisfy your needs. The looseness, the sparkling, the rhythm . . . all right there on the tip of your tongue . . your goal becoming so close that you can almost taste it.

Get in touch with the specific behaviors you will be doing as the real you becomes more and more manifest. See, hear, feel, smell and taste the variety of ways you will be learning to do new things in your life; exercise, cooking, interacting with others, walking, moving, drinking what is good for you. Eating what is appropriate and ecological. So many new and wonderful things to learn.

Explore your environment. What is new there? What kinds of foods will you keep? What kinds of smells and tastes will you notice? What kinds of smells and tastes most represent the new person that you are? What kinds of reminders will you have around you that you can see, hear and feel? Perhaps if you ate more pears you would be able to pare away what no longer fits you, and your "pear shape" would become a "pair shape" that attracts and fits the person you'd most like to pair with. Find anchors for each of your senses. What kind of variety could you add to your environment in terms of color, music and activities that would stimulate and support your new behaviors, capabilities, beliefs and identity?

That's right. And just keep allowing yourself to learn, learn, learn, learn, learn; finding the information you need to be satisfied at each level and through all your senses. And perhaps as you allow yourself to become fully aware of sights, sounds and smells of the room around you . . . your body, the taste in your mouth . . . you can sense the new you fully contacting the present and really enjoy just being yourself.

Mary: Thank you.

Hierarchy Of Criteria Summary

1. Identify a behavior that the person wants to do but stops him or herself from doing, e.g., person wants to exercise consistently.

2. Elicit the criteria that motivates the person to want the new behavior, e.g., person wants to exercise in order to be "healthy" and "look good."

    a. Elicit the strategy and/or submodalities the person uses to decide each criterion, e.g., "health" = Ad/V^c "look good" = V^c

3. Elicit the criteria that stop the person from changing. NOTE: These will be higher level criteria because they override the criteria for motivation, e.g., person does not exercise consistently because there is "no time" and "it hurts."

    a. Elicit the strategy and/or submodalities the person uses to decide each criterion, e.g., "No time" = V^r/K "it hurts" = K

4. Elicit a higher level criterion that overrides the limiting criteria of Step 3. For example you could ask, "What is something that is important enough that you can always make time for it and would do, even if it hurts? What value does that satisfy that makes it more important?", e.g., "Responsibility to my family."

    a. Elicit the strategy and/or submodalities the person uses to decide this criterion, e.g., "Responsibility to family" = V^c/K

5. You are now set up to use one of the following techniques:

    a. *Leveraging.* Apply the highest level criterion to the wanted behavior to override the limiting objections. For example, you might say, "Since your behavior is a model for your family, wouldn't you be showing more responsibility by finding the time to keep healthy and look your best?"

b. *Pacing the limiting criteria.* Find a way to achieve the desired behavior that will match the criteria on all three levels and doesn't violate the limiting criteria. For example, "Is there some kind of consistent exercise program that doesn't take time, wouldn't be painful, and that you could involve your family in?"

c. *Strategy/Submodality Utilization.* Adjust the strategy and/or submodality features of the criteria of the desired behavior to match the strategy/submodality features of the highest level criterion.

ENDNOTES

1. Robert Dilts, Richard Bandler, Judith DeLozier, Leslie Cameron-Bandler, and John Grinder, *NLP Volume I* (Meta Publications, 1979).

7

More on NLP
and Health

Visualization Methods and Ecology

There are programs that have been developed to enhance the beliefs of the patient in his or her ability to get well again and to enhance their treatment as well. Visualization is often a major technique employed in these programs. Given some of the ecological considerations we have expressed in this book, I'd like to offer a little caution about the use of certain methods of visualization for health. Let me explain why. When the stress or illness the person is going through is created or intensified by some kind of internal conflict, certain kinds of visualization processes can intensify the conflict.[1] The method of seeing the white cells as the "good guys" and the cancer cells as the "bad guys" can become a metaphor for the person's internal conflict. It might actually exaggerate the conflict. Unfortunately, almost all our understanding of the immune system is modeled on the metaphor of war.

When my mother was dealing with her cancer, she used visualization in a more ecological way. She visualized the white cells as sheep that were grazing in a field taking care of the overgrown patches of weeds (the cancer cells) that had grown up too high. Her tumor represented grass that had overgrown and needed to be recycled back to create ecological harmony. Think about what a cancer cell is. It's not a foreign invader; it's a part of you that is in many ways identical to your healthy cells. Its program has just gone off kilter. Experiments have even been made showing that sometimes cancer cells will go back to being normal cells in petri dishes. So, when you're working with someone on visualization of health, avoid any reference to "good guy/bad guy" or you may be hooking into an already existing conflict. You want to get the two sides working together and uniting to create a harmonious atmosphere.

Making Visualization Work

Tim and Suzi have been studying visualization processes for twelve years. Before applying NLP filters to visualization, they wanted to know why some people were adept at creating behavioral and physical changes quickly through visualization, while others were unable to produce change after visualizing for long periods of time. For example, one of the students that they had in a stress workshop where they taught visualization techniques had chronic sinusitis. He told them that the ailment had been with him for years and that it was just a part of his life. The student reported later that his sinusitis symptoms suddenly disappeared and he felt great after utilizing the techniques that Tim and Suzi had been teaching. He had practiced the visualization technique for several days. They had similar reports from a number of people that they had worked with. However, there were others who told them that when they visualized a symptom or problem getting better, even for many days, no changes occurred.

At the time, Tim and Suzi were teaching "standard" visualization processes in a variety of ways that they had learned from books.[2] The books were basically outlining similar processes and they eventually summarized what they had been reading into the following visualization process:

1. Know what you want. Use affirmations or other techniques to deal with any internal objections to having what you want.
2. Get in a relaxed, receptive state of mind.
3. Visualize having or seeing what you want in as rich a way as possible.
4. Expect and believe you will receive it.
5. Tell yourself you deserve it.

By applying NLP filters to successful visualizers and contrasting them with non-successful visualizers, Tim and Suzi discovered some important differences between the two groups. First, the people who are successful have outcomes that are congruent with the rest of their desires and meet the well-formedness conditions for good outcomes outlined by Bandler and Grinder.[3] Secondly, successful visualizers generally use different submodalities than do those who were unable to achieve their outcomes.

People who have difficulty making visualizations work are often seeing a dissociated image of themselves doing what they want or having their outcome. Sometimes it's even a small, framed, still picture that is *anything* but compelling. On the other hand, successful visualizers are able to see a fully associated experience of having achieved their outcome. This means that they are seeing what they want through their own eyes, as well as hearing, touching, moving, smelling and tasting their outcome as if it were happening in their present experience. This kind of visualizing results in a positive feeling about the visualization and reinforces practice of the technique.

Response expectancy, the belief that something will

happen as the result of an action, is also important. Those who are successful experience their outcome in the visual, auditory and kinesthetic submodalities of *expectations.*

To create your own submodalities of expectancy, take a moment and think of something that you always do, such as going to sleep at night. Check how you think about that. What internal pictures are you making? Are you saying something to yourself or hearing other sounds? What kinesthetics are involved—feelings of movement or touch?

The non-successful visualizers often code their internal experience in the submodalities of hope or even doubt. To check your own submodalities of hope, think of something you "hope" will happen. You'd like it to happen, but don't know for sure that it will—such as getting a promotion at work, or your spouse remembering your anniversary. Examine your internal pictures, sounds and kinesthetics. The most common kinds of submodalities include fuzzy pictures, dissociated movies, a "questioning" tonality of voice, or multiple representations (pictures of having something and pictures of not having it that are flashing back and forth or that are seen at the same time).

If, when using the visualization process for health or any other outcome you want, you include having a well-formed outcome, a fully associated experience of already having the outcome, plus the submodalities of expectations, chances are that you will be more successful in achieving your goal. Below is a full description of a visualization process that we've found to be useful.

Formula For Behavioral Change

1. Decide what you truly want. It must be something that is within your control and something you do want, not "don't want." Determine how you will know when you have achieved your outcome. What will you see, hear and feel that

will provide evidence?

- What are the positive and negative consequences of getting your outcome? Modify your outcome to take care of any internal or external negative consequences.
- Deal with any reservations you may have about getting your outcome. Write down reasons why you can't have it, allow yourself to fully experience any negative feelings that you might have, and create an affirmation (positive self statement) to release any blocks that you might be experiencing.

2. Get into a relaxed, receptive frame of mind.

3. Think of something that you fully and without reservation expect to happen. Go inside yourself and notice the qualities (submodalities) of your internal pictures; (color, location, brightness, clarity, number of pictures) your sounds and voices; (tonal qualities, volume, pitch) and your feelings (tactile senses, sense of motion, action sense) for expecting that something will happen. Write these qualities down to keep track of them.

4. Fully imagine seeing yourself having achieved your outcome as if you were watching a movie of yourself.

- If you don't like the way it looks, modify it until you do.
- If it looks "right" and you have no reservations about it, step into your movie and imagine that you are now experiencing having your outcome, using the submodalities of expectation.

5. Let it go—tell yourself that you deserve it.

Metaphor

Organ Language and Idioms

One thing you want to pay special attention to when

working with people on health issues is **organ language**: metaphorical statements that people make which refer to parts of the body. It is not uncommon for people to make metaphorical references that relate to specific physiological problems they're having. The unconscious often seems to literally interpret language and to reinforce symptoms "suggested" by the individual in his speech. As an example, one person who was actively involved in transactional analysis (where they talk about "giving strokes") had a stroke.

To make use of this in your work, think of organ language that in some way might correlate with the person's presenting problem, and begin using organ language in your own statements to him. Watch for any physiological shifts in the person that let you know you're getting close to his issue. His unconscious mind will respond to you. Here are some examples of the things you can explore; keep in mind that these are only representative samples.

Skin problems: Did you make a rash decision? Are you itching to get on with something? Is something getting under your skin? Do you feel like you have to scratch for a living?

Ulcer, stomach problems: Is something eating at you? Is somebody or something making you sick to your stomach? Is there something you just can't stomach? Does what you are doing take a lot of guts?

Headaches, neck problems: Is someone or something giving you a pain in the neck? Do you keep running head-on into the same problems? Are you carrying the weight of the world on your shoulders? Do you sometimes feel like you've got a hole in your head?

Weight Issues: Are you "waiting" for something? Are certain parts of you going to "waste"—or "waist," as the case may be? Do you have some heavy problems?

Eyesight: Is there some problem you just don't want to look at? Is there something going on you don't want to see? Do you take a dim view of somebody's behavior? Does it seem like nothing's clear to you?

Constipation: Are you always holding back? Do you have to keep a tight rein on things? Do you hold onto your problems? Does it seem like things never go smoothly for you?

Heart: Is something or someone breaking your heart? Do you suffer one heartache after another? Are you heart-sick about something? Do you find yourself doing things half-heartedly? Are you looking for a change of heart about something?

Hemorrhoids: Does something or someone give you a pain in the butt?

I use the metaphors and organ language primarily as a diagnostic tool. As an example, I worked with a gentleman several years ago who had a very interesting symptom. His blood had been coagulating and had slowed down all throughout his body. He mentioned that he had been "out of circulation" for a couple of years because of his illness and I responded, "Well, blood is thicker than water." He suddenly had the realization that this symptom had started two years ago when he got the news that his daughter was dying of a brain tumor. He had never been able to let go of that painful experience and had taken himself "out of circulation."

I don't think a metaphor necessarily causes an illness; it might be that the illness is, instead, reflected in the metaphor. Either way, the metaphor can provide very important information for you as you are working with someone.

Metaphor as a Context for Change

I had a very interesting experience assisting a lady in her early thirties who had leukemia from childhood. Metaphorically, you can think of leukemia as white cells that refuse to grow up—they won't mature. It means you end up being protected in a child-like manner. They don't know what to do so they just keep multiplying and that creates all kinds of problems. Her situation became complicated when the doctors discovered she also had developed cancer of the colon. The treatment for the colon made the leukemia worse and vice versa, so she was in a real double bind. We went back and did some work around the "want to's." I especially had her check out whether or not she really wanted to be healthy. As it turned out, she had some imprint issues with her mother that made her vow never to grow up. After Re-imprinting and Reframing, we moved on to the "how to's" of what she was going to visualize if her immune system was responding appropriately.

After that work with her, an interesting thing happened. She went to a university hospital to get some special kinds of tests. When they did the initial blood test, she came out with a white count of about 53,000 per unit volume. (normal would be 6,000-10,000) The people doing the testing got very alarmed. She said, "Wait a minute. I'm just under a lot of stress from the trip. Give me some time and I'll change that." The doctors sort of snickered, but she proceeded to do her visualization. About 20 minutes later, she asked them to do the blood test again, and this time it was down to 12,000 per unit volume. They thought they had made a mistake in their testing, and asked her to repeat the test. She said "OK" and stopped doing her visualization. When they repeated the blood test again in 20 minutes, her count was back up to 53,000, they thought the second test had been in error. So she did her visualization again and 20 minutes later the count was back down to 12,000. They repeated the test five times and finally concluded it must be the placebo effect, but my client realized that she was doing it herself. She had found an evidence procedure to affirm that her "how to" was working.

After the tests, her surgeon wanted to schedule her for surgery to take out a significant portion of her colon. She delayed her surgery to do some more personal work. She now had the "want to" and had proved she knew "how to"; the next step was for her to have a "chance to." In working with the unconscious part of her that was responsible for her health, she asked how long it would take to be healed. The "part" seemed to be very congruent—about 16 days.

When she told her doctor, he was upset, but agreed to put off the surgery until she had her chance to work on it. He did want to check her periodically. When he checked her at 10 days he saw no appreciable difference and was concerned because of the danger he felt she was putting herself into by delaying the operation. She agreed to schedule surgery on day 17, but only if he would check her out again first on day 16 to make sure that she still needed it. When he checked her on day 16 there was no trace of the tumor at all. The doctor was surprised and said that her cancer was in remission, but could come back at any time. But remission is a funny concept. I could say my cold has been in remission for five years. All the things that cause colds are still present, but my immune system is preventing them from getting out of control.

I heard from this woman not long ago. She has adopted a child, which means she's stayed well and has every intention of living a long life. She said she had recently been through over six hours of tests. The doctors not only found that she no longer had any symptoms of colon cancer and leukemia but that they could no longer find *any* indications that she had had either of the two illnesses. She said she wanted to thank me for two important beliefs—beliefs that I consider to be the crux of this book. First, for helping her to build the belief that illnesses are a communication, and when you respond to the communication, then symptoms will clear up on their own. When you continue to keep in communication with yourself and your body, you can maintain your good health.

The second belief is that often there are multiple communications as well as multiple causes for illnesses. If you deal with *one* of them, you may not deal with the whole problem. If you keep responding to *all* of your communications, you will eventually get well. I had offered her a metaphor about a mother bird with a nest of babies. They all squawk to be fed at once. If the mother bird feeds one, all the others are still squawking and it seems like you're not getting anywhere. Not only that, if you start to feed the others, the one you just fed will start to cry too. But if you keep a balanced approach in communicating with all these different parts (all the different baby birds), you will eventually be able to feed them all. They'll all grow up and fly away free.

This was an important metaphor given what was happening with the leukemia cells. They were not maturing and were still crying to be fed. It served as a useful visualization as well as a metaphor.

Questions

Man: What are the statistics for success of people working with beliefs using the NLP models you've developed for health related issues? I know you've been working with doctors . . . has any follow-up been done?

Robert: I cannot offer you any specific numbers in terms of percentile points or statistics. One of the difficulties of measurement is that the kind of work we're doing addresses only one element in overall health. Many other elements also go into health.

You will find lots of different responses and results after working with a person's beliefs. In some cases, changing the limiting beliefs is the straw that breaks the camel's back; the last piece in the puzzle; the last element in the critical mass of change necessary for the person to restore his or her health.

I have received reports back from people who have made phenomenal recoveries when they were merely *watching* a demonstration in a workshop. A woman in one workshop had an ovarian cyst that she hadn't told anyone about (including me). When she got home from the training, it was gone. Another time when I was working on a weight issue with a demonstration subject, the person running the video camera changed some beliefs about himself and lost thirty pounds after the workshop. In that same workshop, the person running the other camera wanted to work on improving his eyesight. I wasn't able to work with him directly. However, within three weeks after the program, his eyesight had improved 60%, and a year later his whole prescription changed. He doesn't need his glasses anymore. These are examples of major changes occurring with people when they aren't even having the change work done directly on them. That's one of the nice things about beliefs—they're infectious.

Let me give you some examples of results we've had with people who have experienced the belief work directly. The results to expect depend upon the type and severity of the issue you're working with. I worked with a man in a seminar several months ago who had a severe cancer and I understand that he's been up and down since then. At this time his health isn't doing that well. On the other hand, I've had people who come to me with severe problems, like multiple sclerosis, and they'll get a degree of improvement. Often, after one piece of work, the person will get a degree of change, then plateau out again. A while back I did a seminar demonstration with a woman who had severe arthritis. The sponsors of that training wanted to bring her back in to discuss her changes when I returned for another seminar a year later. They had difficulty scheduling her because she had already made plans to go windsurfing and horse-back riding that weekend—which was a good indication of the changes she had made.

I've had a lot of feedback from people who I have worked with who had weight issues. The changes they've reported have been lasting, long term changes with positive results. Often it takes a change in beliefs for people to be able to adjust their weight to what is right for them.

I've worked with several people who had lupus, a condition where your immune system attacks itself. The first woman I worked with had just recently been diagnosed. Her symptoms hadn't progressed very far. Her blood tests returned to normal after the work. I heard from her after a year and a half, and she's still fine. The other woman I worked with who had lupus had lost both kidneys and was on dialysis. She reported back that her attitude had changed for the better, her relationships with her family had improved and she was doing really well. Of course, she didn't grow her kidneys back.

When first introduced to the belief model, Tim did some therapy with a woman around self-esteem and relationship issues. She had been diagnosed positive for AIDS antibodies, which had been passed on to her by her ex-husband. About three months after the therapy sessions, she returned to the hospital and at that time she tested negative, and still does.

I have many examples of these techniques working well when people I've trained use them, for example. Tim and Suzi had a woman come to them who had been diagnosed as having a malignant tumor of her thyroid. She was convinced enough that NLP could make a difference with the tumor that she put off surgery for a month, even though her doctor was pushing her to have the surgery immediately. After two sessions working with her beliefs, she decided to go ahead with the surgery, even though the tumor seemed smaller. When a biopsy was conducted on the tumor after surgery, they found that it was no longer malignant.

As for the demonstration subjects described in this

book; at the time of its writing, Judy and Mary both lost weight. Tim and Suzi saw Mary recently and report that she is definitely no longer pear shaped! Bill's immune system returned to a fully functional state and after about 6 months his AIDs test changed from positive to negative, much to the astonishment of his doctors, and has stayed that way for two years. After the Conflict Integration with Dee, two cats were actually brought into the seminar room at Dee's request. She held and played with them with no sign of an allergic response.

You know it's going to be difficult to ever find a 100% success rate with any one intervention to a complex system like a human being. What most of us are looking for is to increase our success in helping people resolve health related problems. What kind of success have some of the rest of you found when working with this model?

Kate: This model has greatly impacted my work and I've had amazing results with my clients, but not in every case. That's why I'm here; I want more information on how to work with different kinds of people. About a month ago, I worked with my mom, who had an immune system problem which affected muscle functioning in her legs. By last week, her legs had improved enough so that she could drive again (she hadn't driven a car in over a year).

Ken: I've been working with a woman since a workshop I attended about six months ago when I was first introduced to this model. This woman has really changed. She's been chronically depressed since she was eight years old when she lost her mother. I don't think she had ever been happy until I used the belief change model techniques with her recently. In fact, I could give you dozens of examples where this material has worked dramatically.

Man: Have you worked with any of the universities or institutes that are working in psychosomatics?

Robert: We have been working with the University of Miami, School of Medicine. They have instituted some programs, but I haven't received any statistics back from them yet. As ongoing programs are developed, more statistics should be available. There are variables involved that may not make the statistics look very good anyway. Depending upon the nature of what's happening with the person, their ecology, their family system, their childhood memories and such, a single session may or may not be all it takes to deal with all their issues.

Man: The notion of cancer has different meanings to different people—will you speak more on that?

Robert: Let me use my mother as an example. When we worked with her recurrence of breast cancer, we had to do a lot of work with some popular beliefs and some medical beliefs about what having cancer means. For instance, some people have the belief that cancer causes death. However, it's not really the cancer that causes death, but the breakdown of the immune system; so it's the body's response to the cancer that causes you to die. You don't usually die because of the cancer directly but because your immune system, or other parts of your body, become weak and so broken down that infection can take over or the system can't continue to function.

Some people believe that cancer is a foreign invader and that you have to do something exceptional to get rid of it. Cancer is not a foreign invader. The cells are a part of you. You need to transform yourself to create health—not get rid of something.

Another belief is that many people have cancer at some time or another, and what matters is whether your immune system is healthy enough to take care of it. There are lots of examples of people with spontaneous remissions. The reason they call them "spontaneous remissions" is no one knows how to pinpoint the turnaround.

Sometimes medical beliefs come into conflict with psychological methods for achieving health. For example, in my mother's case, she initially had opposition from some of her doctors. When she told her surgeon about the work we were doing with her internal conflicts, he told her that was a bunch of poppycock and would just drive her crazy. When I tried to explain some of the research and ideas behind our approach, he looked at me and said, "You shouldn't experiment with your mother!" Yet, at the same time the doctors were not offering alternatives. So there are those kinds of issues too. Doctors can be very powerful in their influence over patients and can easily impact their patient's beliefs. The patient is in a very vulnerable place with a major disease. My mother and I recognized that the doctors were positively intended, and they didn't want either of us to act foolishly or build false hope. Rather than reject the doctors, we responded to their *intent*, not their words.

As a result of the work my mother and I did in 1982, she's healthy. These same doctors call her their star patient. She's still healthy and has even made a TV commercial.

When you work with a process like cancer, you're likely to run into various kinds of resistance. In your first session with someone you can't always predict what the resistances to change will be. People can make tremendous gains in certain areas, but because they get resistance in their internal ecology system, their family system, their work system and other places, it makes other areas a lot harder to change.

Woman: Would you say that it's the attitude about the illness that really makes the difference?

Robert: It's not just the attitude or change in belief that's going to make all the difference. Beliefs are one very important level of processes. The person needs to follow through with what they need to do in terms of lifestyle, nutrition, relationships, etc. One of the things about a positive attitude is that it generates those kinds of changes.

Positive attitudes fluctuate over time. Even the person who does a great piece of personal work and changes dramatically is going to have doubts at times. It's a natural human thing to have happen, and the person needs support during those times of doubt. If she gets resistance, rather than support from the important others in her life, it can set her back.

Positive attitudes are not steady states. If you wake up on the wrong side of the bed and have a major fight with your spouse or you have some problems at work, it may feed into your doubts. On the other hand, somebody who makes a major belief change and then opens herself up and gets into new relationships or improves her old ones will reinforce her positive attitude. She'll set up a self-reinforcing loop, so she is constantly, positively reinforced. I do want to emphasize that it takes more than a positive attitude to overcome a major illness. When somebody says, "I've changed my belief and I know I can get well again," but he hasn't changed what he eats, his exercise habits, his relationships at home and at work, I don't necessarily believe that he's changed his belief or will get well. When someone *really* changes a belief, a whole lot of changes take place in his life.

I'd like to make one other important comment here. Changing beliefs is not necessarily a long, arduous, painful process. The fact that it took four days when I was first working with my mother doesn't necessarily mean that it takes four days with everyone or that's what you should expect. Each person will be different in terms of his or her needs.

The person you're working with on a major health issue does need a support system and he also needs positive reinforcement. These things will make a big difference in his ability to make the changes work in the long run.

Man: How do you fit medical treatment into this model?

Robert: Working with beliefs is *not* independent of or in opposition to medical treatment. In working with beliefs you can coordinate with traditional methods, and often the person still needs the medical treatment. Few doctors would argue that positive beliefs about health will physically harm someone, although some may be concerned with "false hope." Let me give you an example of how I coordinated with a physician and a client.

I worked with a lady in her thirties four or five years ago who had cancer of the rectum. There were many long term implications. The doctor who did the diagnosis was recommending a colostomy. This meant that her rectal orifice would be closed off. I told her I didn't think anyone would mind if she got a second opinion.

She got a second, and then a third opinion. The second physician said, "Colostomy! You don't need that. Chemotherapy is the appropriate treatment in your case." The third doctor told her that chemotherapy was wrong because of the nature of her tumor. He thought she needed radiation therapy. When the woman came back to me she was more confused than before because she had received such different responses. I suggested that if she believed in what she chose, it would probably be the best for her. I helped her find the one she could really believe in and she chose the radiation. She did have concerns about the side effects that the radiation might have on the other organs in that same general part of her body.

We did some belief work together and she healed from the cancer well and quickly. What impressed her doctors was the fact that she didn't have any side effects from the treatment. She didn't go through premature menopause, have a suppression of appetite, get depressed or have scarring. The doctors wanted her to write a booklet for their other patients on how she avoided the negative side effects. Incidentally, she's completely healthy now.

Tom: Will you speak more fully about the positive reinforcing loops that need to be in place for people?

Robert: One thing that makes a big difference in a person's ability to recover from life threatening illnesses is having "purpose" and a reason or meaning for living. It's not just her relationship with herself or the images that she has of her goals with respect to her health. A will to live is not just based on having a clear picture of the tumor going away; it has more to do with the *meaning* of having the tumor go away. If your tumor goes away, who will you be then? What will having health allow you to do? I've found it very useful to help the person define his mission in life; if there's no reason for living, why bother to heal yourself?

Michael: I used to work in a hospital. A lot of patients with whom I worked could congruently say, "My life is over; I've accomplished what I was sent here for and it's time to move on." I'm concerned that statement is a function of a belief they have and they're not able to see or consider a future for themselves. What do you think?

Robert: What Michael is saying is that life doesn't go on forever; how do you know when a person is congruently saying, "I've achieved what I'm going to achieve and now my time is over"? Certainly, in dealing with death and dying, there are times when you need to respect that a person's desire to die is appropriate. It could also be that the person believes his life is over because of limitations in his belief system or identity. That identity is indeed finished, but that doesn't necessarily mean that all of his life issues are finished as well. In fact, I find the term "remission" to be a very appropriate one for recovery from life threatening illness. Remissions often come about after a person has established a new mission or a "re-mission."

You can't ever make a decision for somebody as to whether or not he should go on living. Working with NLP and beliefs allows you to go to a different level with the person and say, "I don't know if it's best for you to live or die, but what I *will* do is work to help you become congruent about your wants." Make sure the person isn't dealing with a lot of internal conflicts about whether to live or not. Work to help him deal with any situations or imprints from the past that still create problems for him. In order for a person to make a life or death kind of decision, he has to be very "clear," "open," and "in tune" with himself and the world around him. When he is really congruent, he can make decisions about his options.

Woman: How is working with a belief about health different than a non-health-related belief a person might have?

Robert: The methods for identifying a belief and the tools you use are the same. It appears that often relationship issues, internal conflicts, inhibitory behaviors etc. result in or reinforce physical symptoms. Different states and emotions create different chemical balances in your body and provide the conditions for illness. When you help the person resolve a conflict at the identity level, you often take care of the internal conditions that create the illness.

Fred: Are all illnesses related to beliefs?

Robert: Illness is a function of interactions in your biological and neurological systems. It is a systemic process that is not related solely to any one thing. Some illnesses involve very complex systemic interactions—others are more simple. In fact, some physical problems, like many allergic responses, are stimulus-response phenomena and can be changed using very quick and simple mental processes, as you'll see in the next chapter.

ENDNOTES

1. See the Simonton 1 method, described in Re-Imprinting, Chapter 4.

2. *Creative Visualization*, Shakti Gawain; *Visualization: Directing the Movies of Your Mind*, Adelaide Bry; *The Silva Method of Mind Control*, Jose Silva; *Getting Well Again*, Carl Simonton, etc.

3. See Appendix: Well-formedness Conditions for Outcomes.

8

Allergies

 At the first belief and health seminar I conducted, one of the guest speakers, Dr. Michael Levi (a researcher in the field of immunology and genetics and winner of the World Health Association Award for his definitive work, in the 1950s, demonstrating that viruses are infections) mentioned to me in passing that an allergy was like a phobia of the immune system. That comment intrigued me because it made sense at the intuitive level and meshed with other observations I had been making.

For instance, I had known a number of people suffering from allergies who, when they fell asleep or became distracted, would have an immediate change in symptoms. That indicated to me that there was something operating neurologically as well as physiologically. It is well known that people can be desensitized to allergies or can "grow out" of allergies. I had also observed allergies spontaneously clearing up after a person did a piece of psychological change work. So the thought of allergies operating like a phobia of the immune system seemed to fit well as a metaphor and that thought became the seed of a process I developed for dealing with allergic reactions.

As I thought about Dr. Levi's statement and the fact that there was already an NLP process developed for curing a long standing phobia in a remarkably short period of time, I wondered if the same kinds of principles could be adapted to working with allergic reactions.

I began to apply this thinking to individuals who had allergies to find out what would work and what wouldn't. Initially I worked in conjunction with a biofeedback device that I had developed that measures subtle physical changes.[1] This assisted me in discovering the types of brain processes that were involved with allergies. It was from this research that the three anchor allergy process was developed. Tim and Suzi shortened that technique into the fast allergy process that is demonstrated and explained in this chapter also. The demonstrations that follow were transcribed from taped sessions they did in two separate workshops.

I want to offer a *warning* to the reader at this point. In working with allergies, as with any medical problem, it's important to do so in conjunction with appropriate medical treatment. Some allergies involve or can lead to severe anaphylactic shock and can actually be life threatening. So before you use these techniques, be sure the person you're working with is either under the supervision, or the treatment of, a qualified medical practitioner. (Obviously, this caveat goes with all the techniques described in this book.)

I also believe that since we can influence the immune system concerning allergic responses, these principles could then also be extended to the influence of deeper and more pervasive immune system problems, like cancer, AIDS, lupus, arthritis, and many other systemic problems that involve the behavior of the immune system as a focal point.

Fast Allergy Demonstration

The demonstration that follows was done at the National Association of NeuroLinguistic Programming National Conference held in Chicago, Illinois in 1988.

Suzi: OK, Lynda. You say that you have an allergy to hay and grasses.

Lynda: Yes. I've been tested by an allergist, and I know that timothy grass is the worst, and even when they mow the lawn it bothers me. I have a horse, so being allergic to hay is somewhat inconvenient.

Suzi: I can imagine. If we had a bunch of timothy grass that we were mowing in this room right now, what would be happening to you?

Lynda: First I will swell and drain, then the roof of my mouth itches, and my eyes will get bloodshot and drippy.

Suzi: So, for the purpose of testing, imagine that the grass is here right now. That you have . . .

Lynda: (Goes into the reaction and laughs)

Suzi: OK. (Audience laughs) Stop! Stop! We only want enough to calibrate.

(*To Group:*) She's just demonstrated one of the interesting things about allergies. People can create the response just by thinking about being in the presence of the allergen. There is a story about a turn of the century physician named Mackenzie who was treating a woman who had a violent allergic reaction to roses. He found that if he showed this person a very real looking artificial rose, she would still have the violent reaction.[2] Lynda is also showing us the power of the mind. By just thinking about timothy grass she gets ready to have the reaction that she would typically have.

(*To Lynda:*) How soon do you get this response? It looks like it's pretty immediate, right? If you've been exposed over time, does it get worse?

Lynda: It's immediate, and as long as the allergen is

around, the response will be there unless I take medication. If I leave the situation, my symptoms subside.

Suzi: How long has this been a problem for you?

Lynda: (Pause) Since I was about 11 or 12.

Suzi: So you've had to deal with this a long time, a major part of your life.

I don't know if you know how the immune system works; it's really quite interesting. What's happened with an allergy is that your immune system is overreacting and has become overactive.

It has a number of different kinds of cells with different functions. The macrophage is the cell that would typically take care of anything like hay, grass or dust (an innocuous substance) that you breathe in. These cells are scavenger cells. They look a little like an octopus with long tentacles that reach out and ingest whatever that foreign substance is that might get into the body.

When a macrophage encounters a virus, it ingests part of it but also displays one on top of it like a flag. It's almost like a victory flag that is being held up to alert the rest of the immune system that the body has been invaded.

This flag alerts the helper T cells to possible danger. Their job is to match the niches on the side of the flag that's being held up to the niches that they have on their sides that mark substances as dangerous. If there is a match, they will adhere to the substance and send out a message *immediately* for help from the killer T cells. The killer T cells come rushing in ready to fight. They come to where the flag is being held up and explode the virus by injecting it with a chemical.

Lynda: They explode which cell?

Suzi: They explode the cells that are there at the point where the macrophage has held up the flag. That works out fine if you have a virus or bacteria there, but with an allergy, the killer T cell attacks your own healthy cells. One of the chemicals that is excreted when the cells are exploded is histamine, which creates the runny noses, itches and other things that go along with hay fever.

To recap, the immune system made a mistake about what was dangerous and marked out substances that put the active part of the immune system into action. Once that mistake has been made, and the cell is coded in the body, the immune system will go into action immediately, every single time.

We can thank our immune system for operating in that way. Once a cold virus or bacteria has been marked out, the immune system will act to respond to that danger. It's not very pleasant however, when it goes into action when there is no danger.

(*To Lynda:*) Because your immune system learned that so quickly, that means that it's very teachable. What we want to do now is to teach it a new response. We want to show it that the response it's having now is one that it doesn't need to have. We're going to show it a more appropriate response. We'll be saying to your immune system, "Not this response, *this* response. (Gestures with different hands) Not this; *this.*" So it's just a matter of retraining.

(*To Group:*) We want to do an ecology check before we start.

(*To Lynda:*) If you didn't have this response to hay and grass, what would your life be like? What implications would this have for you?

Lynda: Well, it has decreased over the last 10 or 15 years. So, I think it would continue freeing up energy. And there would just be that part missing. The garbage.

Suzi: Would it have any negative consequences? Is there any reason you *shouldn't* give this up?

Lynda: No, I can't think of any.

Suzi: I mean, it's not like you would want to spend all your time with your horses, and other things would go by the wayside.

Lynda: (Laughing) No. It wouldn't limit the amount of

time I spend. I won't allow it to.

Suzi: Once when Tim and I were doing this process with a fellow who was allergic to grass, we got a different response when we asked this question. He said, "Oh! Then I would have to mow the lawn! My wife has to do it now!"

(*To Group*:) We want to make sure at this point in time that we deal with whatever secondary gain might be there. For example, you might find a child who develops allergies or asthma and gets lots of attention from that. In a case like that, you need to assist that child in having ways of getting attention without the asthma or allergies.

There appear to be no serious ecology issues for Lynda in giving up this allergy; not in what she says or by any non-verbal incongruencies.

(*To Lynda*:) What is like hay or grass that you can be around, and your body *hasn't* made a mistake about? Are there any kinds of grasses, green grasses?

Lynda: What about house plants?

Suzi: OK. You're fine with any kind of green house plants? In other words, your immune system hasn't made a mistake about them?

Lynda: Yes. I'm fine around house plants.

Suzi: What we're going for is a counter example that's close to the substance that's now creating the response; the closer the better.

Go back in the past and be *totally there* with your house plants; *really* there. And I want your immune system to pay *special attention* to how it responds when you're in the presence of house plants and green growing things inside your house. And have your immune system pay special attention to precisely how it is that it does this for you. (Anchors that state) Good.

(*To Group*:) I'm making sure I have a good strong anchor for that counter example. Associate the person into a specific situation before you anchor them.

(*To Lynda*:) Now, Lynda, I want you to imagine there's

a plexiglass shield *all the way* across the front of this room, from wall to wall, protecting you. And *over there*, on the other side of the plexiglass you see Lynda. And you see Lynda with this response that we've just established. (Continues holding anchor) A Lynda whose immune system knows just how to respond appropriately to green things growing indoors. And as you look at Lynda over there, *you know* she has the kind of immune system that knows how to respond appropriately. (Pause) OK. *Now*, I want you, very gently, to put that Lynda over there *in* a situation where she would be around grass; the kind that used to create problems for her—timothy grass. Whatever it is. See Lynda over there, *knowing* that she has *this response* that we've anchored in, *fully available to her.* Her immune system *does* know how to respond appropriately. And you'll notice *that* Lynda changing over there, *as* she's in contact with the grass. And it may seem really strange to you inside to begin with. (Pause) And watch over there for that response, that is similar, *now* to what she has with green growing things. (Pause) OK. *That's* right.

(*To Lynda:*) Now I want you to go out there and gather up those Lyndas and bring them right back into this Lynda sitting here. Come back here with me. Imagine, right now, that somebody's mowing the grass, here in this room. They're mowing timothy grass, and you still have your immune system *totally* intact, operating in the way you want it to be operating. And it knows *just* how to respond appropriately. As you imagine seeing timothy grass—as you're right here with me. (Pause) Just relaxed. (Pause) Mn-hm. That's right.

Now, there will come a time in the very near future, when you'll have an opportunity to be in the presence of timothy grass, hay, or anything of that nature. I'd like you to go to being with your horses and feeding them.

Lynda: OK.

Suzi: And have your immune system pay special attention. It now has the *knowledge* of what the appropriate response is, when you're in that position. (Pause) OK.

(*To Group.*) We're going to let that settle in for a minute. This is a little like when you're doing the phobia process with people. You often have a dubious client for a while who says, "Wait a minute. I don't know what's going on. This *shouldn't* be this easy and this *shouldn't* be working that well."

Do you have any questions of Lynda and her experience of this?

Man: When you were imagining that you were in the presence of the allergen, was there any sensation at all?

Lynda: Just a tiny little bit. Sort of like in the back of the center of my face, if that makes any sense. That's all I got that would be like what I normally get. It was like the very beginning of the old response, and then it didn't follow through.

Woman: What was the reorganization of your immune system like to you?

Lynda: It was very much like a collapsed anchor. It is like you can feel things being rewired. Something's happening.

Suzi: That's a wonderful description of it. This *really* does reach down deeply in her neurology for change.

(*To Lynda:*) Now that it's settled in, imagine like you did when we first started out—that you're whiffing in a *big giant whiff of timothy grass.* (Pause, softer) And notice what happens inside. (Pause) Now try hard to get that old response back. (Softer) As hard as you can. (Pause)

Lynda: I'm still on guard, waiting for something to happen. (Laughing)

Suzi: Shock. *Can't you do better than that!* (Laughing)

(*To Group.*) For those of you who were calibrating, was that the same response we got *before* doing the process?

Audience: No.

Suzi: Now, she's still on guard, and rightfully so. She was 11 or 12 when this started. She's still waiting for the response because that stimulus had brought it about every single time.

(*To Lynda:*) And you'll be *pleasantly surprised* when you go out there and wait for that old response, and say, "Oh, it's not here. I can just enjoy my horses when I'm with them."

Lynda: Mm-hm.

Suzi: (Softer) Nothing else needs to happen out there. And you can thank your immune system for being so responsive to learning new ways.

Lynda: Thank you.

Suzi: That process is very easy for you to do with yourself. You said that you were allergic to lots of different things.

Lynda: Yes, there are a few other things too; that was the biggest.

Suzi: Now, if you're a person who *generalizes easily*, I wouldn't want you to *think of the other things that this might also work with.*

Lynda: (Laughing) OK.

Suzi: Have your immune system go through the process automatically for you . . . so that you don't have to do it consciously. Because . . . you know, we learn very quickly, and there's no reason why it couldn't go ahead and do the process with those other substances, so that you don't even have to bother.

Questions

Woman: What if the other person doesn't know what the substance is that they're allergic to?

Suzi: Obviously, it's much harder to find the appropriate counter example if you don't know what the allergen is. With hayfever, when a person only knows that it's "something in the air," try using flour or dust or lint floating in the air for the counter example. You can also use the air at other times of the year when the person responds appropriately.

Man: Some people are allergic, in testing, to virtually everything. But there are some times when they respond to the allergen and other times when they don't. What's that about?

Suzi: That might mean that the allergen is very stress related, and it deals with their emotional state. That lets you know that there's another piece that needs to be in your intervention; teaching them how to respond differently in the situation that creates stress. For instance, do any of you who have hayfever notice that some years it's far worse than others? If you look back, it might be because of what was going on in your life—not that the pollen count is any different. Your internal state makes a difference.

Man: What do you do if it comes back?

Suzi: If they re-create it somehow, do it again. It typically only takes five minutes to do. Also double check the appropriateness of your counter-example and ecology, especially beliefs that might be in the way. Occasionally you might have to do a re-imprinting or a conflict integration.

Woman: Have you used this with children?

Suzi: Yes. It works well with children. The youngest one we've heard of it being done with was about 3 years old.

Man: What if the process doesn't work?

Suzi: Perhaps the person was not using the appropriate counter-example. The closer the counter-example is to the allergen, the better. Take for instance an allergy to cow's milk. Can the person drink goat's milk or soy milk? If they're allergic to all kinds of milk, is there something white and liquid that the person is okay with, like coconut juice, or something like that? I find it's better to have the person come up with their own counter-example, rather than me choosing it, but suggestions are often helpful.

Another primary reason that it doesn't work has to do with secondary gain and ecology. The ecology issues might not come up at the beginning of the process—you may not catch it until you're having the person do the future pace. You may need to do reframing, new behavior generator, re-imprinting, change personal history etc. to deal with the secondary gain first, before proceeding with the immune system.

Thirdly, there can be an underlying imprint that is the real root of the allergy. It never hurts to check for an unresolved imprint experience before doing the allergy process with someone. That way you can be really *thorough.*

Woman: Have you used it with life-threatening allergies?

Suzi: Yes, and if you were my client with a life threatening allergy, I'd insist that you agree to go to a doctor to have an appropriate medical test to validate medically that you no longer have a reaction. If you're dealing with a severe case of allergies with either life-threatening or terribly unpleasant symptoms, you may want to use three place dissociation . . . as if it were a phobia. The purpose is to get the person far enough removed that she won't collapse back into the symptoms.

Fast Allergy Process Summary

1. **Calibrate**. Ask, "What's it like for you when you're in the presence of the allergen?" Watch for the person's physiology, eye accessing cues, breathing, etc.

2. **Explain the mistake of the immune system.** Explain that her immune system has made a mistake about something being dangerous when it really wasn't. The immune system has marked out something as dangerous that's not, in and of itself. It can be retrained rather quickly.

3. **Check for ecology/secondary gain.** What would her life be like without this? Are there any positive or negative consequences? Use whatever NLP techniques you need to at this point to deal with ecology issues before proceeding.

4. **Find an appropriate counter-example resource.** Find

a counter-example that is as similar to the allergen as possible; that the immune system responds to appropriately. Anchor that response and then *hold that anchor throughout the whole process.* Make sure the person is associated as you set the anchor. If possible let the person come up with her own example of what is similar.

5. **Have the person dissociate.** Using a plexiglass shield from wall to wall is an easy way to establish dissociation. *While holding the anchor,* have her see herself over there on the other side of the plexiglass having the resource. Use all your fluffy language suggesting that she is "the *you* you want to be," and that her immune system operates appropriately.

6. **GRADUALLY, introduce the allergen.** As she is watching herself over there behind the plexiglass, have her slowly introduce the allergen, *the thing that used to create the problem.* Introduce it as a gradual process giving her the opportunity to get used to it. **Wait, at this point, until you see a physiological shift.** It's like the immune system says, "All right, I've got it. I'll change the notches on my flag so it doesn't match up with any of the T cells I have."

7. **Reassociate.** Bring her back into her own body and have her imagine she is in the presence of the allergen as you continue to hold the resource anchor.

8. **Future pace.** Have her imagine a time in the future when she will be in the presence of the thing that used to create an allergic response for her.

9. **Test.** If you can actually test carefully on the spot, do that. If not, re-calibrate to see if the physiology, eye accessing cues, breathing, etc. have changed.

Three Anchor Allergy Process Summary

This is the process that Robert Dilts first began utilizing when he was working with allergies. The only difference between the preceding technique and this one is that this process utilizes three anchors simultaneously (one for dissociation, one for the counter-example, and a resource anchor), instead of just one counter-example.

1. Calibrate.
2. Explain the mistake of the immune system.
3. Check for ecology/secondary gain.
4.

    a. Have the person dissociate, and anchor the state of dissociation. This is added reassurance that you can keep the person dissociated.

    b. Find an appropriate counter-example re-source and anchor that. This is the same as the other process.

    c. Ask the person how she wants to feel when she's in the presence of the allergen. This might be "the *you* you want to be" in that situation. Anchor this re-source also.

5. Use all three of the anchors set in Step 4 to have the person see herself with these resources available.
6. Gradually introduce the allergen in the dissociated state.
7. Let go of the dissociation anchor and have the person reassociate having the other two resources still available.
8. Future pace using the two resource anchors.
9. Test.

Foreground/Background

The next pattern we want to discuss is called the Figure/Ground or Foreground/Background procedure. Robert developed this technique after reading about some of Pavlov's experiments with dogs.[3]

I'm sure you all recall that Pavlov was the Russian scientist who conducted a lot of the initial studies on stimulus-response phenomena. In one of this studies, he conditioned a dog to salivate when it heard a bell, a buzzer and a tone all at the same time. Pavlov found that each of the sounds had a different value in getting the dog to salivate. The bell might get ten drops, the buzzer five and the tone two. In other words, the bell was in the "foreground" of sounds the dog heard, i.e., the dog paid more attention to the bell than to the buzzer or tone. The tone with the least value would be background.

Pavlov found that if he then inhibited the dog's response to the tone so the dog didn't salivate at all when he heard the sound of it (so it had a value of zero), then reintroduced the tone with the bell and buzzer, the value of the combined sounds would fall to zero. The combined three sounds no longer served as a stimulus for the dog to salivate.

This same principle can be applied to allergies and other stimulus-response problems people have. You can use the Foreground/Background technique when you have a specific stimulus in a defined context. It's been used on phobias, on unpleasant reactions to the sound of a dentist's drill, negative responses to unpleasant voice tones, etc.

Foreground/Background Demonstration

Tim: Does anyone here still have an allergy?

Gary: I am allergic to cottonwood trees. When their fluff is blowing, I get congested. The thing that's interesting about it is that when I pay attention to my symptoms, they get worse. When I get involved in something, they aren't as bad.

Suzi: Good. Maybe we can assist you in *really* noticing other things.

Tim: What's it like for you when you're around cottonwood trees?

Gary: (Displays tension around his eyes and his skin

color becomes uneven.) My eyes begin to itch and my nose gets congested.

Tim: If there was cottonwood fluff around now would it bother you?

Gary: Oh yeah.

Tim: Do you like pine trees? I'd guess you're OK in a pine forest. (Kinesthetically anchors Gary's arm as he begins to think about pine trees.)

Tim: (Abruptly, while still holding the "pine tree" anchor) What do those tennis shoes feel like on your feet? (Creates an association between any sensations in Gary's feet and what it's like for Gary to be around pine trees.)

Tim: (Releases anchor) How about cottonwoods? If you were walking among the cottonwoods . . . what is it like?

Gary: (Confusion, blinks several times, shift in state to the physiology associated with pine trees) Wait a minute . .

Suzi: It's called burning out the circuits.

Gary: It's like a shock. (He sits quietly for a few moments.)

Tim: What's it like for you now when you think about cottonwood trees? Can you get any of the old response back?

Gary: . . . No.

Suzi: Well just see the room full of those little white fluff balls.

Gary: . . . I'll try harder. (Exhibiting none of the physiology he displayed earlier when he thought about cottonwoods.) When I go back in my mind to the past, when I've had the reaction, it's like it's never been there. That's what's weird.

Tim: (*To Group:*) This is a process that is easy to do covertly since it goes so fast. The applications for family therapy, business interactions and couples work are probably obvious since it works on visual or auditory anchored responses.

Suzi: (*To Group:*) Let me explain what Tim did with

Gary. The cottonwoods were originally foreground in Gary's perception. His feet, which are always present with him, were background.

Tim: So we created a strong association between his feet and a counter-example (pine trees) that he has no immune reaction to. As long as the pine tree counter-example is close enough to cottonwood trees in his way of thinking, the technique will work.

Man: How would you do it covertly?

Tim: That *was* covert to anyone not familiar with anchors. Another example occurred the other day when I was talking with a man wearing a coat and tie. He was telling me how he was having trouble with his wife and how she'd nag at him when he called her from work. I assumed he had a negative anchor to her voice tone in the context of nagging. Later I told him I was glad I didn't have to wear a tie and asked him if he minded wearing one. When he accessed whether or not he minded, I anchored the response visually by holding an imaginary tie knot in my collar. I then asked him about some conversations he had with his wife when he *really* was interested in what she was saying, while firing off my visual anchor of holding the imaginary tie knot. Then I asked him about her nagging and he had a very different response than he did the first time he mentioned her nagging. He said it probably wasn't that bad after all. He had no conscious idea what happened, but I'm sure his unconscious mind approved, as I know his wife will when he starts listening to her.

The important thing is to find a counter-example that's "close enough" in the person's way of thinking to generalize. The best kind of counter-example is when a person should have had the response they're complaining about, but didn't. For example, I could have asked Gary if he'd ever been around cottonwood tree fluff and didn't have the allergic reaction. The next best counter-example is something that the person considers in the same category of things (trees, in Gary's case) or behaviors (conversations in the example of the man with the tie).

Suzi: When we first saw Robert work with this, he was working with a woman who felt anxious when she heard a dentist's drill. Robert asked her for a counter-example . . . something that sounded like a dentist's drill but that she had no reaction to. She thought of an electric mixer. The technique didn't work with that counter-example. It turned out that a critical element was that *she* controlled the mixer and the *dentist* controlled the drill. Barber's shears later worked fine for the counter-example. It sounded similar and the hairdresser controlled them.

Tim: It's even better when the counter-example is something the person enjoys. The woman said she enjoyed having her hair done because she was doing something that made her feel more attractive. Some of those good feelings carried over to the dentist context.

For the background element you can select something that will always be there . . . temperature, sensations in the hands or feet, etc. Be a little careful about what you select and check it out with the person first. We were working with a man who was allergic to cigarette smoke. His wife smoked, so he had a big problem. We used his feet as the background element, like we did with Gary and he suddenly had an unpleasant reaction. It turned out that he used to smoke, but quit when his doctor said he had circulation problems in his feet!

Foreground/Background Process Summary

1. Identify a limiting response that occurs in a specific context (an allergy, the sound of a dentist's drill, an annoying voice tone).

    a. Calibrate to the physiology associated with it.

    b. What is foreground? What are they most aware of?

2. Find an appropriate counter example resource. Either a time when the person should have had the response, but didn't, or a similar context that is like the limiting one.

    a. What is foreground? What is the person most aware of?

3. Identify something that must occur in both the limiting context and in the counter-example that is outside the person's conscious awareness. What is background in both? (i.e., the way the soles of the feet feel, the weight of their clothes, etc.) *Anchor* this feature.

4. *While holding the anchor,* have the person focus on what she is most aware of in the counter-example experience. Your goal is to create a strong association between what is most in her awareness (foreground) and something that she is not attending to (background).

5. Release the anchor and immediately have the person remember and associate into the previously limiting experience.

6. Calibrate to the physiological response.

    If the limiting response still occurs, recycle through Step 3 with a different counter-example and strengthen the association between the foreground and background features.

7. Future pace by holding the background anchor while the person thinks of future contexts.

Mapping Across Submodalities Process Summary

There is a way that you can use counter-examples and submodalities in working with allergies. Instead of using anchoring, you find out what submodalities are present when the immune system is working appropriately and map those across to where you have an inappropriate response. Often you will find that there is one critical submodality difference.[4]

1. Calibrate.

2. Explain the immune system's mistake.

3. Check for secondary gain/ecology issues.

4. Find an appropriate resource/counter-example. Elicit the submodalities for that counter-example. You can ask, "How do you think about it?" These are the submodalities the person's immune system uses when it's responding appropriately.

5. Elicit the submodalities associated with the allergen situation. These are the submodalities the person's immune system uses when it's responding inappropriately.

6. As the person thinks about the allergen, have him map across the submodalities so that it matches the submodalities of the counter-example.

7. Future pace.

8. Test.

ENDNOTES

1. The Mind Master is a sophisticated biofeedback device designed to work with an Apple 2 or IBM PC computer. It contains several biofeedback games and other very useful programs. It is available from Behavioral Engineering, 230 Mt. Hernon Road, Santa Cruz, California 95066.

2. John N. Mackenzie, "The Production of the So-Called 'Rose Cold' by Means of an Artificial Rose," *American Journal of Medical Science, 9*, (1886): 45-57.

3. *The Essential Works of Pavlov* (New York, New York: Bantam Books, 1966).

4. See *Using Your Brain for a Change*, Richard Bandler, 1985, Real People Press.

Epilogue

One of the core beliefs and promises of NLP is that effective thinking strategies can be modeled and utilized by any individual who wishes to do so. A large portion of this book was drawn from modeling the strategies and beliefs of people who had effectively recovered from potentially debilitating or life threatening illnesses as well as other mental and physical issues regarding well-being. The same principles may be applied and utilized in other areas of human excellence. For example, Wolfgang Amadeus Mozart is considered to be one of the greatest composers of music in all human history. As we mentioned earlier in the book, perhaps what sets Mozart apart from others is not mysterious mystical talent, but rather a very real and concrete strategy he used for organizing and integrating his experience. He utilized his strategy in a way that allowed him to excel to the degree that he did. I have studied letters of Mozart and found he actually laid out a fairly explicit and yet extremely elegant creative thinking process that I modeled. That process can be used to create harmony in areas other than simply musical notes. The following is a meditation for health that is drawn from the formal thinking process used by Mozart to compose music. Even though the content has to do with internal experience, health and vitality, the structure of this psychological symphony is drawn from the master himself.

Exercise

Allow yourselves to take a moment and just be aware of your bodies . . . be aware of feelings . . . perhaps there are parts of you that you haven't really paid attention to very much during the day . . . notice the symmetry of your hands, your body, your feet, your left side to your right side . . . and then . . . pay attention . . . deeply inside of yourself . . . find a part of yourself that you've always been able to trust to be healthy . . . that, in spite of whatever illnesses you've been through, you've always been able to count on this part of you . . . it's part of your body.

Maybe it's your heart. Maybe it's your eyes. Maybe your lips. Maybe your legs. Maybe your ears. Find a part of you that, when you think about it, always feels vital, always seems healthy. The part of you you *most trust* to stay healthy and to stay vital. (Pause.)

And as you put your awareness on that part, as you really go into that part, *feel it.* Feel that part of your physiology, of your body. (Pause) And, as you do, begin to imagine that this part of your body is like a musical instrument. And it makes a sound, a noise, a melody. And listen to the sound of those feelings . . . the sound of that part of your body that incorporates within it your vitality, your energy. And listen to that sound. And as you hear the sound, perhaps you can make the feeling stronger, and the sense of health and vitality and aliveness can begin to spread beyond that part of your body. (Pause.)

And as you hear that sound and feel that feeling, perhaps as you take your next breath, you can smell that sound. You can smell that sense of aliveness, of vitality. And notice what it smells like to you. Is it sweet or is it fruity? Is it spicy? Is it aromatic? And notice what that smell is like inside. And what taste it might have. So that you can smell and taste that sense, the feeling of vitality. (Pause.)

And let that smell and that sound begin to spread. And think of any parts of your body, and other feelings that might not be as healthy as you'd like them to be. And listen to the sounds and the tastes of those parts of you, as if they were part of a meal . . . like part of a symphony . . . a piece of music. And begin to allow the sound and smell and taste of that life and vitality and health to serve as a counterpoint, or a dance, with all the parts of your body. So it spreads through from the insides. And even begin to see it, as if it were light spreading from that part of your body. What color, what brightness would that energy, that vitality look like, as it dances in rhythm . . . in colors . . . in the music . . with all of the other parts of your body spreading from the inside out. Massaging from the inside every part of your body. (Pause.)

And know *that* music and *that* dance can continue. Even through tonight in your dreams, in your sleep, in the back of your mind . . . that music can spread . . . that light can spread its warmth, its flavor all through you. And that you can taste that, in the things around you, in the food that you eat. In the sights that you see and the sounds that you hear. And that the sounds of life and health, and the colors of life and health, and the tastes of life and health can be there for you. And if you can pay attention to those, your unconscious mind can lead you to what are the most appropriate things to eat, to see, to hear. (Pause.)

And perhaps that light within you can become so strong and bright that it begins to shine out through your pores and eyes. And the sound spills out through your tone of voice, and spreads to others, without your having to try, but just by people being near you. They feel it, and they sense it. (Pause.)

And allow that process to continue at its own pace, its own rate of speed, in the way that's most ecological for you. And any of the ideas or the learnings that you've made here today, know that you can accept or incorporate them, or consider them, in a way that's most ecological and appropriate for you.

And tomorrow morning, when you wake up, may you arise with a sense of energy and vitality, a relaxed feeling but with an alertness *that* perhaps you can feel as you allow your eyes to open and make contact with the world around you here. And even noises from outside the room won't interfere with that sense of inner vitality and peace.

BIBLIOGRAPHY

Anderson, Jill. *Thinking, Changing, Rearranging: Improving Self-Esteem in Young People.* Portland, OR: Metamorphous Press, 1988.

Andreas, Steve and Connirae. *Change Your Mind and Keep the Change.* Moab, Utah: Real People Press, 1987.

Bandler, Richard. *Using Your Brain—For A Change.* Moab, Utah: Real People Press, 1985.

Bandler, Richard, and John Grinder. *The Structure of Magic I.* Palo Alto, CA: Science and Behavior Books, 1975.

Bandler, Richard, and John Grinder. *The Structure of Magic II.* Palo Alto, CA: Science and Behavior Books, 1976.

Bry, Adelaide. *Visualization: Directing the Movies of Your Mind.* New York: Harper & Row, 1979.

Dilts, Robert. *Applications of Neuro-Linguistic Programming.* Cupertino, CA: Meta Publications, 1983.

Dilts, Robert. *Roots of Neuro-Linguistic Programming.* Cupertino, CA: Meta Publications, 1976.

Dilts, Robert, Richard Bandler, Judith DeLozier, Leslie Cameron-Bandler, and John Grinder. *Neuro-Linguistic Programming, Vol. I: The Study of the Structure of Subjective Experience.* Cupertino, CA: Meta Publications, 1979.

The Essential Works of Pavlov. Ed. Michael Kaplan. New York: Bantam Books, 1965.

Gawain, Shakti. *Creative Visualization.* Berkeley, CA: Whatever Publishers, 1978.

Grinder, Michael. *Righting The Educational Conveyor Belt.* Portland, OR: Metamorphous Press, 1989.

Kostere, Kim, and Linda Malatesta. *Get The Results You Want.* Portland, OR: Metamorphous Press, 1989.

Lee, Scout. *The Excellence Principle.* Portland, OR: Metamorphous Press, 1985.

Lewis, Byron, and Frank Pucelik. *Magic of NLP Demystified.* Portland, OR: Metamorphous Press, 1982.

Silva, Jose. *The Silva Mind Control Method.* New York, NY: Simon & Schuster, 1977.

Simonton, Carl, and Stephanie Matthews-Simonton. *Getting Well Again.* New York: Bantam Books, 1982.

Stone, Christopher. *Re-Creating Your Self.* Portland, OR: Metamorphous Press, 1988.

Taylor, Carolyn. *Your Balancing Act: Discovering New Life Through Five Dimensions of Wellness.* Portland, OR: Metamorphous Press, 1988.

GLOSSARY

ANCHOR: Stimuli that will consistently produce the same internal data in an individual. Anchors occur naturally. Bandler and Grinder discovered old modeling that you can deliberately set-up a stimulus with a gesture or a touch or a sound to hold a state stable. Where an external stimulus is paired with an internal state.

AS IF: A method using "pretend" to behave "as if" something is true. Used to create a resource.

ASSOCIATED STATES: States where you are experiencing an event "in time" as though it is happening now, in your own body, looking through your own eyes. Full involvement in the moment or fully reliving a past experience.

CALIBRATION: Using sensory acuity (see, hear, feel) to notice specific shifts in a person's external state, i.e., voice tone, posture, gestures, skin color, muscle tension, etc. to know when changes are occurring in their internal state.

CHANGE PERSONAL HISTORY: An NLP anchoring process that adds resources into past problem memories.

CONGRUITY: When all parts of you are in agreement about your behavior in a particular context.

DISSOCIATED STATES: Being in the position of mental observer to your own action; watching yourself through the eyes of the observer.

EYE ACCESSING CUE: Eye movements that correlate to visual, auditory or kinesthetic thinking.

FUTURE PACING: Associating a person into the future where an external cue in their environment will trigger an internal response or specific behavior. Once the brain has rehearsed a process in this way, the behavior will automatically be available in that future context.

INCONGRUITY: When a person is in some kind of internal conflict and two different messages are being sent. External behavior and internal feelings don't match and often show up as asymmetry in the person's physiology.

IMPASSE: A smokescreen. When a person draws a blank or gets confused as you are working on an issue with them.

META-MODEL: 17 language distinctions that are used to gather highly specific, sensory based information.

META-PROGRAMS OR META-SORTS: Habitual thinking processes that people use to sort information and make sense of their world.

NEW BEHAVIOR GENERATOR STRATEGIES: A process where a person reviews a situation where they don't behave as they would like to and then adds new resources into that situation. They can either (1) choose a resource that they have had access to in the past; (2) pretend like they have the resource, or (3) find someone else that has a resource and model them.

OUTCOME: An end result that has defined sensory based evidence for achievement.

PACING: Matching or mirroring another person's behavior, including their posture, tone, tempo of voice, breathing, predicates, etc. (See Rapport)

PART: A complex of behaviors or a strategy, i.e., "There is a part of me that wants me to lose weight."

PSEUDO-ORIENTATION IN TIME: To reorient someone in the past or future.

RAPPORT: Being on the same wave length with another person; being "in sync" with them. Rapport occurs when you are matching or pacing another person's behavior on a variety of levels.

REFRAMING: In NLP terminology, a redefining process where secondary gain as the intention behind a behavior is validated. It changes a person's perspectives and provides new choices.

REPRESENTATIONAL SYSTEM: The internal and external pictures, sounds, words and feelings that we use to "represent" and make sense of the world.

SENSORY ACUITY: The skill of watching, listening or kinesthetically sensing minimal cues another person offers you in his/her analogy.

STATE: Bringing together all a person's thinking processes at one time to create a set of thinking processes that directly affect the physiology.

STRATEGY: A sequence of internal representations (pictures, sounds, words, feelings) that lead to an outcome.

SUBMODALITY: A modality is a term that references one of the five senses, i.e., visual, auditory, kinesthetic, etc. A submodality is a component part or quality of a modality. For example, in the visual modality, submodalities include brightness of a picture, clarity, focus, size of picture, associated vs. dissociated, etc. Auditory submodalities include tone, pitch, volume, tempo, duration of sound, etc. Kinesthetic submodalities include pressure, extent, duration, etc.

SWISH PATTERN: A generative NLP submodality process that programs your brain to go in a new direction.

TRANSDERIVATIONAL SEARCH: Commonly called the T-D search. A process where a feeling is anchored, and utilizing the anchor, the feeling is taken back in time to other times the person has had that same feeling.

VISUAL SQUASH: A process of negotiating between two internal "parts" or polarities that includes defining the parts, identifying the positive purpose or intention of each and negotiating agreement with resultant integration.

APPENDIX A

OUTCOMES: WELL-FORMED CONDITIONS

I. What do you want?

    A. What will having that outcome get for you?
    B. Is the outcome:

        1. Stated in the positive (what you *do* want, not what you don't want)
        2. Can it be initiated by you?
        3. Can it be controlled by you?
        4. Is it a large global outcome or is it or manageable chunk size? Chunk down into smaller pieces if necessary.

II. How will you know when you've got it? (Evidence procedure) Is the evidence described in sensory based terms? (see, hear, feel, smell, taste)

III. Where, When, and With Whom Do You Want It? (Context)

IV. What stops you from having your outcome now?

V. What are the positive and negative consequences of getting your outcome?

VI. What resources do you need to get your outcome? (Information, attitude, internal state, training, money, help or support from others, etc.)

VII. Is the first step to achieving your outcome specific and achievable?

VIII. Is there more than one *way* to get your outcome?

IX. What time-frames are involved?

X. Imagine stepping into the future and having your outcome fully. Look back and determine what steps were required to achieve the outcome now that you have it.

INDEX

*Index created by Dale L. Longworth
Re-edited by Mellanie Collins*

ROBERT DILTS

Mr. Dilts has been an author, developer and consultant in the field of Neurolinguistic Programming (NLP) since its creation in 1975 by John Grinder and Richard Bandler. A long time student and colleague of both Grinder and Bandler, Mr. Dilts also studied personally with Milton H. Erickson, M.D. and Gregory Bateson.

Recognized internationally as one of the foremost trainers and practitioners of NLP, Mr. Dilts has done consulting and training throughout North America and Europe to a wide variety of professional communicators and organizations. He has also lectured extensively on NLP including presentations for Harvard University, The US Festival, and The California Association of Special Education Teachers.

He is the principle author of *Neuro-Linguistic Programming, Vol. I,* which serves as the standard reference text for the field, and has authored two other books and a number of articles and monographs on NLP.

Mr. Dilts has a degree in Behavioral Technology from the University of California at Santa Cruz. He received the President's Undergraduate Fellowship in 1977 for research correlating eye movement and brain function conducted at the Langley Porter Neuropsychiatric Institute in San Francisco.

Since 1981, Mr. Dilts has been President of Behavioral Engineering, a computer software company that uses NLP concepts to create interactive computer products for education, training and personal development. He is the author of over two dozen computer programs, including *Mind Master,* a unique computer interface that allows the computer to input and respond to a person's thought patterns.

TIM HALLBOM

Tim Hallbom co-founded Western States Training Associates/NLP of Utah LC in 1981. Since then, he has provided practical, skill-based training to individuals, businesses, and government organizations through-out the United States, Europe, and Latin America. A certified NLP trainer, co-author and therapist, Tim served as the President of the International Association of NLP from 1991-92.

Tim has been involved with NLP since 1980 and is the co-author of the audio cassette, "How To Build Rapport." He is also featured in the video, "Eliminating Allergies" and the Nightingale-Conant audio tape series, "NLP—The New Technology of Achievement." Moreover, he has published several NLP articles for various magazines and journals, and contributed a chapter on NLP and Health for the medical encyclopedia, "Alternative Medicine."

Through his knowledge of NLP and the mind/body/spirit relationship, Tim has helped many people around the world who suffer from various conditions such as cancer, multiple sclerosis, arthritis, migraine headaches, allergies, and many more. He also has extensive experience in public counseling positions, including clinical social work services to battered spouses, volunteer programs, and the Utah State Department of Social Services. He also served as an adjunct faculty member at the University of Utah and Weber State University.

Tim received his Masters in Social Work from the University of Utah in 1972. Since then, he has spent thousands of hours researching stress, health, and personal productivity. He has been actively involved in communication and behavioral change related training since 1979. He also maintains a private psychotherapy practice in Salt Lake City.

SUZI SMITH

Suzi Smith has been studying the relationship
between people's behavioral patterns and health since
1979. As an international NLP trainer, she has devoted
her life to teaching people how to have more personal
control over their health and well-being.

Suzi has been actively involved in personal productivity training since 1978. In 1981, she and Tim Hallbom
founded Western States Training Associates/NLP of
Utah LC, through which they provide training and
consulting to a wide variety of individuals, businesses,
and government organizations. She currently continues to conduct
training sessions throughout the United States, Latin America, and
Europe.

She has been using NLP since 1980 and has met the rigorous
standards to become a certified NLP trainer. She also served as the
Western United States Regional Representative for the International
Association of NLP for three years. Because of her vast experience in the
field of NLP and health, Suzi has helped many people around the world
who suffer from an array of physical conditions such as allergies, TMJ,
cancer, multiple sclerosis, eyesight problems, and many others.

Suzi received her Master's Degree in Counseling from Virginia
Polytechnic University in 1976. She is the co-author of the audio cassette,
"How To Build Rapport." She is also featured in the video, "Eliminating
Allergies" and the Nightingale-Conant audio tape series, "NLP—The
New Technology of Achievement." Suzi has also authored numerous
articles for the NLP publications, *Anchor Point* and *NLP Connection,* and
she has been featured in several different newspapers and magazines
throughout the United States.

For information regarding training opportunities contact:

Strategies of Genius
P.O. Box 67448
Scotts Valley, CA 95067-7448
TEL (408) 438-8314
FAX (408) 438-8314

Western States Training Associates
NLP of Utah LC
346 South 500 East #200
Salt Lake City, Utah 84102
TEL (801) 534-1022
FAX (801) 532-2113

PERSONAL NOTES

Goals

"Goals are dreams with deadlines."

PERSONAL NOTES

Action Steps

"Shovel while the pile is still small."
John Klovas

PERSONAL NOTES

Progress Diary

*"Thinking well is wise; planning well, wiser;
doing well wisest and best of all."*
Persian Proverb

PERSONAL NOTES

Ideas

"Minds are like parachutes—they only function when open."
Lord Thomas Dewar

_____

_____

_____

_____

_____

_____

_____

_____

_____

_____

_____

_____

_____

_____

PERSONAL NOTES

Gift List
Friends to send "Beliefs" to:

Representative Titles Available From
Metamorphous Press

BUSINESS
Performance Management
Michael McMaster
Learn how human group systems work—or don't work—and how to create the conditions for change in a business organization. Four book set combined into one volume. ISBN 1-55552-041-3 PB

CHILDREN
Thinking, Changing, Rearranging: Improving Self-Esteem in Young People
Jill Anderson
Helps young people gain control over their inner states and behaviors. Over 300,000 copies in print. ISBN 0-943920-30-2 PB

EDUCATION
Righting The Educational Conveyor Belt, 2nd Edition
Michael Grinder
A comprehensive workbook for educators, outlining NLP techniques for classroom management and teaching excellence. All levels. ISBN 1-55552-036-7 PB

ENNEAGRAM
The Enneagram Spectrum of Personality Styles
Jerome Wagner, Ph.D.
This comprehensive introductory guide outlines the nine different "hues" of the Enneagram: the virtues, passions, shifts, and paradigms of each of the personality types. ISBN 1-55552-070-7 PB

HEALTH/FITNESS
Beliefs: Pathways To Health & Well-Being
Robert Dilts, Tim Hallbom & Suzi Smith
Leading edge technologies that rapidly and effectively identify and remodel beliefs which affect health. Learn how to change unwanted beliefs and habits into lifelong constructs of wellness. ISBN 1-55552-029-4 PB

HYPNOSIS
Training Trances
Julie Silverthorn & John Overdurf
How to therapeutically communicate with the unconscous mind, using an integration of Ericksonian techniques, traditional models of hypnotherapy, and recent research in related areas. ISBN 1-55552-069-3 PB

PSYCHOLOGY/NLP
Magic of NLP Demystified
Byron Lewis & Frank Pucelik
One of the bestselling introductory NLP books—offers clear, understandable explanations of NLP principles with illustrative graphics, charts, and glossary. ISBN 1-55552-017-0 PB

RELATIONSHIPS
NLP Made Easy
1—How To Build Rapport
Introductory information on rapport within relationships by the co-authors of *Beliefs: Pathways To Health & Well-Being*. Single cassette. ISBN 1-55552-044-8
2—Understanding Communication Styles
An overview of NLP. Offers you the opportunity to hear the communication categories in action. Single cassette. ISBN 1-55552-045-6

SALES
Sales On The Line
Sharon Drew Morgen
Questioning strategies which create rapport by approaching sales from the perspective of the buyer rather than the seller. Powerful for any environment where communication is involved. ISBN 1-55552-047-2 PB

THERAPY
The Enneagram and NLP
Anné Linden & Murray Spalding
By therapists and for therapists, this compendium describes the Enneagram personality styles in a clear fashion, while incorporating the latest strategies to make the changes in life that you desire. ISBN 1-55552-042-1 PB

These are only a few of the titles we offer. If you cannot find our books at your local bookstore, you can order directly from us:

Metamorphous Press
P.O. Box 10616   Portland, OR 97296-0616
TEL (503) 228-4972
FAX (503) 223-9117

TOLL FREE ORDERING
1-800-937-7771

Call or write for our free catalog, prices and availability, shipping/handling charges, or other information.

Printed in the United States
57225LVS00002B/301-312